THE EXIT-STRATEGY PLAYBOOK

THE **DEFINITIVE GUIDE TO**
SELLING YOUR BUSINESS

THE EXIT STRATEGY PLAYBOOK

ADAM COFFEY

LIONCREST
PUBLISHING

THE EXIT-STRATEGY PLAYBOOK

The Definitive Guide to Selling Your Business

ISBN   978-1-5445-2304-0   *Hardcover*

       978-1-5445-2303-3   *Paperback*

       978-1-5445-2302-6   *Ebook*

       978-1-5445-2305-7   *Audiobook*

This book is dedicated to the multitude of people across the globe who made my first effort, The Private Equity Playbook, a bestseller. Without your desire to expand your horizons, The Exit-Strategy Playbook would not have been possible. Your direct outreach and engagement inspired me to keep going, to push harder, and to accelerate my efforts to give back to the business community for the many blessings I have received throughout my career.

CONTENTS

INTRODUCTION

It's about that time. You're a successful entrepreneur, but you're wondering if there is a light at the end of the tunnel. You're becoming more conservative. You're not as young as you once were. Bad economic news causes stress. You see other businesses getting hammered by COVID-19, and you lament the stories shared by other founders at Rotary, business mixers, or the American Legion Hall: "If I had only sold sooner." You're wondering if you're going to be in business for the rest of your life.

I've seen these feelings many times over in the constellation of companies I've bought through the years. These are normal feelings; they're early indicators that it is time to *do* something. But what is that something?

That's what we're here to figure out.

SALES PROCESS ONE HUNDRED TIMES OVER

I refer to myself as a blue-collar CEO. I left home at seventeen years old, right after graduating high school. I enlisted in the United States Army, which taught me about discipline, teamwork, and leadership and set the foundation for the rest of my career.

After military service, I worked as an engineer for a number of years, which made me a meticulous planner. Eventually, I crossed over from engineering into business and worked for ten years at General Electric, where I moved into mid-level management and learned how to run a company.

Private equity recruiters came knocking on my door, and I launched into a twenty-year career, serving as the president of three different companies. The businesses were all in different industries. One was a medical company, Masterplan, that serviced imaging and biomedical equipment in hospitals. Another was a commercial laundry firm, WASH Multi-Family Laundry, that serviced 550,000 washers and dryers located in 70,000 apartment complexes and laundromats across North America. The third business was CoolSys (pronounced as two syllables, "cool sis"), America's largest specialty refrigeration and HVAC service company, touching more than 50,000 different customer locations.

All three were national private equity-backed companies that I helped grow by using a tactic known in the industry as *buy and build.* I start with a platform company that's owned by a private equity firm, and then I buy several other companies and combine them to build a larger company. In the four years I've been at my current company, I've purchased eighteen smaller companies and have three more under letter of intent as of today. Over the next four years, I'll probably buy a grand total of fifty. When I'm finished, the company will sell for somewhere between $2.5 and $3 billion in enterprise value.

This process will continue with the next owner until the company eventually hits the public markets anywhere from five to ten years from now.

As a result of the positions I've held, I know how to buy and sell companies and successfully work through the sales process. I've become an investor in private equity funds and an advisor to others. I am frequently asked to look at businesses and offer opinions from an operational perspective. In sum total, I have bought, sold, and financed around one hundred companies in twenty years. The individual company values ranged from under $1 million to over $1 billion, with an aggregate total amount of financial activity measured at close to $5 billion.

I've dealt with dozens of entrepreneurs who were selling their companies, so I can definitely help you sell yours. I understand how this game is played.

SELLING YOUR BUSINESS IS AN ART

I get it. You're an expert in your field. You are an entrepreneur who established a business and then continued to grow it for decades with your personal sweat equity. You've built an empire, and you are potentially a multimillionaire, but this is no time for pride. Selling isn't just a big deal; it's an art, and it takes years of experience to gain expertise. For many reading this book, this is the first time you have looked to sell. You are going to need help. Good news: I am an artist here to guide you step by step!

In my first book, *The Private Equity Playbook*, I primarily focused on private equity. What is it? How does it work? How has it grown over time? Who are the players? What do they do, and how do they seek out companies to partner with? How do you pick a good partner? Then finally, how do you plan to grow a business once it is a part of your portfolio?

This book is the companion to that book. You may ultimately decide to sell to a private equity firm, and if that's the case, you should definitely pick up that book! But that's not the purpose of *this* book.

Here, you're going to learn about all the potential buyers of your established business. You're going to learn the process of preparing a company for sale. Hopefully you're starting this process years before you actually want to sell because there is a lot of prep work ahead of you.

But don't let that work scare you. At the end of the day, this prep work will not only accelerate a transaction when it's time to exit, but it will also maximize the value that you receive at exit.

A QUICK NOTE ON PROFESSIONAL ADVISORS

This book is not intended to provide financial advice or legal advice, steer you in a particular direction, or answer all your questions. Rather, it will help you if and when you ever decide to sell your company.

Note: You'll want to always employ the expertise of your team—attorneys, accountants, investment bankers, and more—because the legal, financial, tax, accounting, and other business issues that you will face are very based on facts. The outcome of your sale will be impacted by laws, rules, and regulations—federal, state, and local—the interpretation of which will be dependent on those facts. Therefore, the advice that you need can be provided only by experts who know the details of your life (especially your personal goals), your business, and the proposed transaction. Now is not the time to "save" on assembling your team of advisors, as we will discuss in Part Three. This book is merely a primer to help open your eyes to some of the many intricacies that you will encounter when seeking maximum value at exit. It will prepare you for the journey ahead and demystify the process so you can navigate it with better confidence and clarity.

HERE'S WHAT WE'LL COVER

This book assumes you are the owner of an established company with real revenue and earnings. This is not about the world of VC-backed adventures, although there are certainly nuggets of wisdom for those entrepreneurs as well. It is organized in four parts.

- Part One: The Universe of Buyers and Exit Strategies. Here, you'll learn about the types of buyers who may be interested in your company and the pros and cons of each.
- Part Two: Prepping Your Business to Sell. In this part, you'll learn what you should be doing years ahead of your sale, including cleaning up your financial reporting, dealing with any real estate the business owns, and aligning operations.
- Part Three: Build Your Advisory Team. Your advisory team is critical to obtaining maximum value from your sale. You'll learn why you need a tax advisor, accountant, lawyer, and investment banker, and I'll show you how to find them!
- Part Four: The Sales Process. Find out exactly what the typical middle-market sale process looks like—from start to finish.

The reason I've meticulously organized each step is that ultimately this book isn't about selling fast—it's about selling smart and achieving maximum value.

Are you ready to learn more? Let's get started.

PART ONE

THE UNIVERSE OF BUYERS AND EXIT STRATEGIES

You have spent years building a business, and you're now starting to think about an exit strategy.

Meet my brother Mike. Mike is the real-life embodiment of the two characters from my first book, Rose and Josh. Rose was a mid-level *Fortune* 500 employee who left to run a company backed by private equity. Josh was an entrepreneur who sold a plumbing company to private equity. Like Rose,

Mike had a first career in corporate America and rose to the executive ranks of a large insurance corporation. In 2005, Mike and I bought an insurance agency together, and he launched into a second career as an entrepreneur, like Josh. As Mike got older, he faced the age-old question: when is the right time to sell? Mike is an absolute expert at all things insurance. But 2020 was his first time selling a business.

And guess what? There were sharks out there just waiting to buy his business, and they can detect in a matter of minutes who is a sophisticated seller and who is not. Luckily, Mike was able to sell to an excellent large strategic buyer that allowed him to stay on and become a rollover investor (topics we will cover later in great detail). But what about you?

There are many types of buyers and exit strategies out there. You need to find the best fit based on *your* future goals. Do you know the different types? Do you know how to spot them and how to understand if they are a fit or a waste of time? Do you know what their needs and goals are based on type? Do you know which one is the best choice for your situation? If you answered no to any of these questions, stay tuned!

CHAPTER ONE

↓

STRATEGIC BUYERS

We're going to start with strategic buyers because they are one of the two most common type of buyers you'll encounter. A strategic buyer is a company that seeks to grow by purchasing another company. The strategic company might be a public company, a private company owned by an individual, or a private company owned by private equity. The acquiring company's backing and structure are irrelevant. How the acquiring company pays for the purchase is also irrelevant—it may be some combination of cash, leveraged debt, seller note, or stock. The key thing to note is that the buyer type remains strategic when a financial entity or institution does *not* make the purchase—rather, one company purchases another.

When Morgan Stanley bought E*Trade, Morgan Stanley was a strategic buyer. When Facebook bought WhatsApp, Facebook was a strategic buyer. When Amazon bought Whole Foods, Amazon was a strategic buyer. Get the picture?

Strategic buyers purchase for a multitude of reasons, including:

- Expanding into a new geographical market or customer vertical.
- Building density to create saturation in existing markets.
- Buying expertise, knowledge, or new technology.

Strategic buyers are typically larger in size than the companies they seek to acquire but not always. Sometimes little guys buy big guys too! In general, though, the reason big guys buy smaller guys is that along with size comes the ability to generate enough internal cash or raise enough debt to successfully make the purchase.

In the end, the strategic buyer makes the purchase in order to gain customers, market share, geography, and expertise. There is generally a specific strategy that drives them to acquire, and thus the term *strategic buyer* was originally coined eons ago by someone my research was unable to uncover!

TYPES OF STRATEGIC BUYERS

I like to say there are two types of strategic buyers: those that want to *turn the lights off* and those that invite you to *join the team.*

TURN THE LIGHTS OFF

This type of buyer is not necessarily interested in your expertise. They want your customers and are buying density.

Let's say one plumbing company services Phoenix, Arizona. They are looking to build density by adding customers in their existing geographic market and customer vertical, so they purchase another local plumbing company. They already have a president, finance department, service staff, parts, and everything they need. They are only looking to increase the size of their existing business and don't need another CEO or HR department. For that matter, they are not even expanding into new geographies, so they most likely won't even need the other company's offices or warehouses.

Although my example above is small in nature, you often see this playing out in larger corporate mergers with many markets that overlap across broad geographies. After the acquisition or merger closes, there's a period of integration. They make a number of cost reductions and increase profits, and the benefits of the strategic acquirer become fully realized. This concerted effort is known as *harvesting the synergies.* They may offer the second business owner a consulting agreement to stay on for a period of time. They may offer bonuses to keep key individuals on during the transition. They may keep some of the staff—drivers, service technicians, or other types of worker bees—but the rest are dismissed. One company more or less displaces the other. They literally *turn the lights off* in all the offices of the acquired company at some point post acquisition.

When I was the CEO of WASH, our normal mode of operation was to acquire companies, work with the founders under a consulting arrangement, and then jettison the majority of the overhead cost of the business. If the geography overlapped, everything would go in the back office and warehouses. Only the people working in the field were kept on. We did this approximately thirty times in my thirteen-year tenure. The only exceptions were when we entered new geography or countries. In those cases, more people retained their jobs, but in virtually all cases, relationships with former owners and founders lasted for only brief periods of time. This company was mostly buying density and access to new markets and the existing long-term contracts and relationships. The primary strategy of the company fit into the category of *turn the lights off*.

JOIN THE TEAM

As the CEO of CoolSys, I have bought eighteen companies over the last four years, and sixteen of eighteen owners—and the overwhelming vast majority of all acquired employees—

are still active in the business. So what happened to the other two owners? They retired, which was their original goal in selling. This is the opposite of a company that wants to turn the lights off. This strategy is known as *join the team* or *keep the lights on.*

The primary key drivers of my using a different strategy at CoolSys are as follows. First, the industry that CoolSys plays in has contracts that, regardless of length, can be canceled with thirty days' notice by either party. At WASH, we acquired contracts that weren't cancelable and lasted, on average, five to seven years. Although relationships were important to WASH, the fact that customers couldn't leave meant that we had time to build new relationships before contract renewal. We only needed the entrepreneurs long enough to help us facilitate that transition.

The second reason was that I had a scalable platform at WASH, and the industry had very predictable ways of conducting business. I could fully and easily integrate companies we acquired. At CoolSys, we are still investing in our technology platforms, and customer interactions are very different depending on the geographic market and specific vertical. The end result is that we need and want entrepreneurs to stay and become a part of CoolSys for a much longer time period or even permanently.

As seen above, an acquiring company may choose to *turn*

the lights off or *join the team* based on their own individual strengths and weaknesses. At CoolSys, I am purchasing a relationship, so the goal is to retain the owners who created the relationship. I want them to be a part of the company, help us retain their employees, and in essence, *keep the lights on.*

DETERMINE YOUR IDEAL BUYER

As you begin to entertain possible buyers of your company, it's important to understand what type of company you'll be dealing with. You can catch the potential buyer's deal team off guard and get honest answers by asking overtly.

Start by asking, "How many companies have you acquired in the last five years?"

If they've purchased fifteen companies in the last five years, you can ask, "How many of those former entrepreneurs are still active within the business today?"

In my case, I would respond, "Sixteen out of eighteen owners; two have retired." That is a very good indication that I'm a person who is not turning the lights off and who will invite you to join the team.

If they tell you that you are the first company they are acquiring, you can then ask more directly, "What are your post-close plans for my company?" or "What is the strategic rationale behind your desire to purchase the company? Is this a buy and build? Are you turning the lights off on my business or am I joining the team?"

These questions will show you are a savvy and knowledgeable seller who is capable of an elevated and more meaningful conversation. Buyers will be less apt to attempt to lowball you or play games.

WHEN DO YOU CONSIDER A STRATEGIC BUYER?

If your company is too small to serve as a platform company with a financial buyer (discussed in Chapter Two), you should consider selling to a strategic buyer. The universe of financial buyers will be limited due to your size. This could mean selling to a small private equity firm buyer, or it could mean selling as an add-on company to a strategic buyer. You may decide that it's safer or easier to be part of a larger company or that you want to learn from the structure of a larger organization.

My brother Mike and I ultimately sold our insurance agency in January 2020 to Acrisure, a multibillion-dollar company. We chose this strategic buyer because my brother was getting close to retiring and wanted to diversify his holdings, but he wasn't quite ready to retire yet, so he also wanted someone who would keep the lights on. There were some minor synergies harvested, but my brother continued in his role. He was able to roll over some of his stock and is now an investor in Acrisure (more on rollovers in Chapters Two and Twelve). He's also running the same company with the same employees—just now under the umbrella of a much larger organization.

Sometimes a strategic purchase can be very positive for the seller because they now have a greater sense of security and strength in the new size and numbers. Our insurance agency wasn't big enough to be a platform company for a financial buyer, and because insurance agencies are generally slower-growth annuities, financial buyers wouldn't pay any kind of premium price for the company. There was no question that a strategic was the right solution for us, and in Mike's case, one that would keep the lights on was absolutely the right buyer!

At CoolSys, the original business owners still aggressively run their businesses, but now they make better business decisions because they are part of a very large organization that can help them think about opportunities, provide capital funding, and work through any issues.

During the early days of the COVID-19 crisis, we held daily calls with all of our entrepreneurs and senior leaders. They felt safer as part of a team. Had they been part of a small independent company, they would have been on their own and wondering what moves to make. Several of them reached out to me to say, "I was really glad to be part of something bigger during lockdown when business appeared to be tanking. It was nice to have friendships and a group of people who had insights I might not have had."

WHAT IS YOUR POST-CLOSE FUTURE WITH A STRATEGIC BUYER?

Let's say you're older and want to retire now. If that's the case, a strategic buyer that wants to turn the lights off is a potentially perfect fit because you get your escape and can head off to the lake to fish every day after a brief transition!

However, if you're younger and want to diversify but not necessarily exit, a strategic buyer that keeps the lights on is a great path to contemplate.

Those are the biggest elements to consider. Are you seeking a short-term consulting agreement that you can then leave, or are you seeking to work for a period of time and remain partially invested? By remaining partially invested, you can see second paydays and receive another bite of the apple (more on second paydays and bites of the apple in Chapter Two).

NOTE: DRIVING UP PRICES

In a sale process, strategic buyers can usually pay the highest price for a company due to their ability to model synergies, integrate businesses, and eliminate duplicate cost. Because the sum of the parts can be more valuable than the two companies independently, the strategic buyer has an edge over other types of buyers when it comes to price.

This advantage gap has been narrowing greatly over the past decade. The inflow of capital to private equity—more than $4 trillion, with $1.5 trillion in committed cash looking for companies to buy *right now*—has financial buyers paying very high prices. I'd argue that in today's market, there is virtually no discernable difference between the two, and in many cases, I see the tables turning in financial buyers' favor.

That being said, having a few strategic buyers in the mix of potential buyers will help you drive up the price of your sale and achieve maximum value. It keeps the financial buyers on their toes so they won't play games! One potential downside is time, especially if the strategic buyer is very large or public. Generally, large public strategic buyers move very slowly. They are the battleships, and the small strategic or financial buyers are the speed boats that can navigate to a closing table quickly.

KEY TAKEAWAYS

- Strategic buyers can often pay the highest price because of synergies—whether they choose to harness them or not.

- Strategic buyers may or may not be in your best interest if you want to stay on as a part of the company.

- It's always good to have a few strategic buyers in the mix for competition and to keep the financial buyers honest.

- Strategic buyers may be platform companies owned by private equity with the goal of executing a buy and build roll-up strategy where they combine a lot of companies.

- Large public strategic companies may move slowly.

CHAPTER TWO

↓

FINANCIAL BUYERS

A financial buyer is a person or a firm deploying capital to buy a self-contained company with the intention of growing that company and using it as a platform.

A financial buyer cannot lay off the management team because they don't have their own team to run the company! The purchase is truly an exercise in financial backing. The seller gets some liquidity at closing and generally needs to stay on to keep the company running. A financial buyer will also want to see the former owner roll over a portion of their proceeds to reinvest in the business. This demonstrates commitment to the new owner's success by "putting their money where their mouth is."

The financial buyer brings the checkbook—not the machine.

In my career, I have held the role of CEO for three financially owned platforms. Using the buy and build strategy, I built those companies from enterprise values of $100 to $250 million up to enterprise values of $500 million at the first exit and up to $1 billion at the second exit. In all three cases, I saw multiple financial owners come and go during my tenure.

As a seller, I see financial buyers far more than I see strategic buyers. As the CEO, I became a strategic buyer of many companies while I built the initial company for the financial buyer of the platform. I'm a strategic buyer because I'm a company buying a company, even though my backing is from a financial buyer. Understanding these nuances is key.

Entrepreneurs tend to use organic growth as a primary driver. Financial buyers tend to purchase a platform company and then grow both organically and by using the buy and build strategy.

WHAT IS PRIVATE EQUITY?

At the time of this writing, the latest private market data indicates that there is over $4 trillion in capital and assets under management in private equity, up from approximately $3 trillion when I wrote *The Private Equity Playbook* just a few years ago. Money continues to flood this alternative asset class, and over 50 percent of all companies sold involve a private equity group on at least one side of the table. Often, once you get into enterprise values in excess of $100 million, you'll find private equity on both sides of the table.

In just two years, the number of private equity firms has grown from 5,400 to more than 6,000. Financial buyers have quickly become the most predominant buyer of all companies. When I go through the process of selling a company I've built, I may have thirty potential buyers, two of which are strategic and the rest are financial.

There is an urgent need for private equity to put money to work. With $4 trillion in assets under management, of which $1.5 trillion is in committed cash, everyone is out looking for something to buy *right now*.

BUT WHAT *IS* PRIVATE EQUITY?

Think of it like a mutual fund.

A mutual fund aggregates a pool of money from a number of investors. A fund manager decides what investments to purchase, how long to hold them, and when to sell. The funds have readily available liquidity and are publicly traded. If you want to purchase a mutual fund, you hop onto your investment account and buy a piece of it. That money is then aggregated with everyone else who has contributed.

You can hold that investment as long as you want—for one day or five years—but you have no say over the trades made by the fund manager.

Morningstar is the most common rating system that people view for comparisons of mutual funds. A five-star fund outperforms a four-star fund for the same time period. Morningstar ranks the fund managers (and the funds themselves) based on the funds' performance.

Private equity is like a private mutual fund in that it aggregates money from large-scale investors. The typical minimum investment size is $5 million, often from pension funds, college endowments, or high-net-worth private individuals seeking to diversify investment opportunities. These private funds are then used to purchase companies or buy stakes in companies. Much like the mutual funds, the people who invest in private equity (the limited partners) have no decision-making authority over the firm or the investments the fund makes. The private equity firm serves as the general partner and controls the investments.

The stock market, over a thirty-year period, offers approximately a 7 percent return annually, on average. Private equity as an asset class has averaged nearly double that amount, at around 14 percent. Top-quartile funds typically generate returns above 20 percent, while lower-quartile funds are lucky to keep pace with the stock market. As long as private equity fund averages beat the broader stock market averages, this alternative investment class will continue to grow at a rapid pace—it has and it is.

WHAT'S THE DIFFERENCE BETWEEN A MUTUAL FUND AND PRIVATE EQUITY?

Liquidity.

Mutual funds are liquid. Private equity is not.

Limited partners pledge capital for a specified amount of time, generally the life of the fund, and thus cannot buy and sell on a whim.

A private equity fund has a charter of about ten years. The limited partners commit capital, and then as the firm makes investments, they ask investors to send in their pro rata portion of the equity required to buy the companies. Over this ten-year fixed life of a fund, the limited partners have no control over liquidity. The money early on is used to purchase companies. During the middle years of the fund's existence, the firm works to improve and grow the companies and do add-on acquisitions. The firm may call for additional capital during this time period. In the later stages of the fund's life, the firm sells the companies in order to return all of the capital and proceeds back to the original limited partners to meet that ten-year timeline horizon.

*Note: There's much more to private equity. This is a quick over-
view, but for more information, please read* The Private Equity
Playbook.

FIRM SIZE AND BUYER SIZE

With thousands of firms out there, you'll find many financial
buyers in all size categories. Most medium- to large-sized
firms have multiple funds while small firms or micro firms
may have only one main fund active, with a second fund
winding down or just starting up. The good news is that
they are all out there looking for you! There is always a
firm of the appropriate size to buy virtually any company
that is for sale.

I define the firm sizes as follows:

- Boutique/micro firm: funds under $100 million.
- Small firm: funds under $1 billion.
- Midsize firm: funds $1 to $3 billion.
- Large firms: funds $3 to $10 billion.
- Mega firms: funds higher than $10 billion.

Small boutique firms buy small companies. They may
have less resources than big firms, but most small firms
are started by people with large-firm experience who know
the private equity game. These firms tend to have a more
intimate feel about them. The risk to a small firm is their

more limited resources when it comes to executing some specific strategies like buy and build.

Larger funds typically have the capacity to execute any strategy that arises, but they only buy larger companies to serve as platforms. Thus, a small entrepreneur can't typically sell a small company to a giant firm.

Like in many things, there is a right-sized tool for the job. You can estimate the right financial buyer size to target based on some simple math.

Let's assume your company has $5 million in EBITDA (earnings before interest, taxes, depreciation, and amortization, discussed in Chapter Four). If your company is in an industry that trades for ten times EBITDA, the expectation is you need a buyer willing to pay $50 million in total for your company ($5 million × 10 = $50 million). If an average private equity transaction in your industry uses five times the leverage or debt, then the purchase will be made with a combination of $25 million in debt financing and $25 million in equity. If the average private equity fund buys ten companies per fund, then the right-sized financial buyer typically has a fund of 10 × $25 million—or at least $250 million!

As a seller, you can use these calculations to estimate the size fund, and thus the size firm, of your target financial buyer. But you don't have to do this math and go hunt for firms. In

Part Three, we are going to assemble your team of advisors. It's their job to do all of this for you—and you absolutely need a team if you intend to earn maximum value at exit.

ROLLOVER INVESTMENT AND SECOND BITE OF THE APPLE

As part of my current buy and build adventure, I paid $16 million for the first company I purchased as an add-on to my platform. The owner took $12 million off the table to diversify his personal portfolio and rolled over $4 million into CoolSys, the parent company. I was a platform company owned by a financial buyer, but I was also a strategic buyer, keeping the lights on.

Approximately thirty months later, I sold CoolSys for four times the return on investment. That seller who rolled over $4 million got another check for $16 million. Instead of selling his company one time and riding off into the sunset, he sold the company, worked actively, and in total, got $28 million for a company he would have been perfectly content selling for a one-and-done price of $16 million. ([$16 million first bite – $4 million rollover] + $16 million second bite = $28 million.)

Most entrepreneurs would have chosen not to roll over any of the proceeds from the first sale. They say, "If I don't own the company, I don't want to invest in it." But private equity firms are very successful. If they can beat the market index by a magnitude of two, they don't generally make bad decisions. As an entrepreneur, you should take that into consideration. You can ride the coattails of very sophisticated investors by making a rollover investment in order to get a second bite at the apple.

We'll discuss this more in Chapter Twelve, but I introduce it here because it is part of the beauty of working with private equity—either by having them as the financial buyer *or* by having them as the financial backing of a strategic buyer (as with CoolSys) that is keeping the lights on. The math works the same either way. You won't make any more or less if you are a platform or an add-on. The question is one of risk diversification. When you are the add-on to a strategic, your risk is spread out among all the companies the strategic platform buys. When you are bought by a financial buyer and become the platform, the risk is entirely yours based on your execution. There is no right or wrong, better or worse. Both buyer types can get the job done for you and model similar returns for their investment.

WHEN DO YOU CONSIDER A FINANCIAL BUYER?

You'll want to consider a financial buyer when you are seeking to diversify your own personal assets, but you're not necessarily ready to hang up your cleats. Yes, you could potentially join the team with a strategic buyer, but you will definitely have the opportunity to stay on with a financial buyer.

With a financial buyer, you remain an independent company. Private equity wants you to be a part of a firm's fund portfolio that they will purchase and use as a platform investment— an anchor holding of their fund.

WHAT IS YOUR POST-CLOSE FUTURE WITH A FINANCIAL BUYER?

In Chapter One, we discussed how strategic buyers fall into one of two categories: turn the lights off or join the team. In the case of strategics, you are destined to become part of a larger organization. You may call the shots on specific strategy, but in general, you are bound to conform to the desires of the collective.

With financial buyers, the overwhelming majority would like to see you stay. These buyers brought their checkbooks, but they are really investing in you. You spent decades building a business and you're the expert. The buyer is just backing you and working with you to ramp up your growth. It's always easier to be more aggressive when you have a partner with a massive capital structure and a desire to grow.

Financial buyers will work hard to help you succeed. You'll employ creative strategies to accelerate growth. It's not unusual for me to enter a company that is growing at less than 10 percent annually and bend the curve to make it grow at 30 percent annually.

Don't worry, though. If your real goal is to exit stage left, just be open and honest. Let the financial buyers know it's time to hang up your cleats, but you are committed to helping them transition the business over a period of twelve to eighteen months and are willing to be both a rollover investor and consultant to help the new CEO be successful. Although financial buyers want you to stay, they are realists, so it won't kill the deal. In Part Two, we will talk a bit about how to position yourself for that eventuality.

KEY TAKEAWAYS

- Financial buyers are typically private equity firms because they have so much capital that needs to be deployed. They have an urgent need to go out and find companies to buy.

- Financial buyers want you to stay. They just provide the checkbook.

- Financial buyers want you to roll over a significant piece of the equity so that your interests are aligned and you have skin in the game.

- Financial buyers typically use you as a platform to drive future growth.

- A competitive sale process with multiple buyers and types represented yields maximum value for sellers.

CHAPTER THREE

ALTERNATIVE BUYERS

The majority of the purchase deals done today are with either strategic or financial buyers, as we've already covered. However, there are other types of buyers. In select circumstances, those types of buyers may be even more attractive than a strategic or financial sale.

OWNER-OPERATOR

Imagine you are a dentist and have owned your practice for forty years. You've decided you want to retire. A younger dentist can transition in and work with you for a year or two before you transition out. Then they become the owner-operator of your company on a go-forward basis.

Owner-operator sales are common for small service industries—legal practices, financial planners, dry cleaners, medical practices, plumbers, electricians, landscape companies, and so forth. The typical purchase is an up-front down payment with financing over time as the company continues to bring income to the new owner. That financing could be in the form of a seller note, private financing, bank or commercial loans, or some combination thereof.

Remember that insurance agency my brother Mike and I purchased? We bought it from an owner-operator. He chose to provide some of the financing. My brother came in stage left, and the owner exited stage right, but there was a continuity to the business. The seller held back a note, and we paid him 10 percent interest annually for five years. We also offered him a consulting agreement, so he was able to monetize the business and generate income in multiple ways.

Note: Just because you own a business in one of these industries does not mean your only option is an owner-operator. All of these types of businesses have large strategic buyers currently active in the marketplace today. Due to the rise of private capital and private equity, virtually any company can find a viable strategic or financial buyer. No matter who you are, there's somebody rolling up your industry. I promise you that a large privately or financially backed company is investing in dental practices, specialty doctors, veterinarians, insurance agencies, and more.

Over the last couple of years, I have also seen a hybrid version of owner-operated businesses that marries owner-operated and financial buyers. This relatively new and growing format is called a *search fund*. A search fund is a small financial buyer that partners with a businessperson, often a recent MBA graduate with some business experience, who goes and searches for a small company to buy and run. This type of buyer is typically making a lifestyle choice to pivot from a nine-to-five desk job working for someone else to being the business. The investors are banking on the experienced businessperson's ability to grow the business, and they supply the capital to make the purchase. Search funds typically back the new owner-operator who is looking to buy something in the $5 to $50 million price range and might need $2 to $15 million in equity.

MANAGEMENT-LED BUYOUT

A larger company may have a management team that decides to do a management-led, or management-leveraged, buyout (MLBO). These are typical when the team is sophisticated and helped grow the business, and they decide to lead the buyout of the company from a retiring founder or owner.

A traditional MLBO makes use of the capital of one or more members of the leadership team to pull together resources and come up with a down payment to buy out the entrepreneur. They then obtain financing for the balance due—similar to a mortgage on a home. That financing could be from a seller-held note, a bank, the Small Business Administration, and so forth.

In this instance, the buyers don't give up any equity to purchase the business. The minute they give up more than 50 percent of the equity to a financier, they are now financial buyers that got a proprietary deal. Likewise, if they give up more than 50 percent equity to another company, they just became a strategic buyer. In my book, MLBOs are only MLBOs if the management team maintains control.

I see this type of buyout frequently when a business has multiple generations working within the company. The first generation may be nearing retirement age and need some liquidity—thus the need driving the sale—but they don't mind holding back a note or working with the buyer group to help facilitate their needs. This is a friendly transaction and generally includes a large element of trust between parties.

Even in these cases, though, buyers still need the help of experts to make sure that the terms are market and the sale price is fair. Although I won't discuss MLBOs in detail in this book, it is still a sale, and expert advice helps ensure buyers are not taken advantage of by a friendly seller. In these situations, I often see nonstandard terms being dictated by Mom, Dad, and their advisors—not because they are being devious, but rather because they simply have no idea what is reasonable and customary.

EMPLOYEE STOCK OPTION PLAN

Another less common potential buyer or exit strategy is an employee stock option plan (ESOP). ESOPs (pronounced as two syllables, "e-sop") were all the buzz decades ago when they first launched but are not very common today. In fact, in the United States, out of more than ten million companies operating, only 6,717 are ESOPs.

ESOPs typically fall into one of two categories. The first is an altruistic owner who wants the employees to own the company. In this category, the owner sells the company to the employees, and the company/employees take out a loan from a bank to provide the liquidity needed, along with some tax-advantageous elements for the seller—namely, an ability to defer taxes on the money received or any financing note held. The cash flow from the company finances the debt. If there is an excess of profits, the ESOP makes distributions back to all of the employees who are now the owners of the company. Over time, the ESOP pays off its debt and makes regular distributions to all employee shareholders.

I have also seen ESOPs used in a second category: when a seller simply cannot find a buyer for any multitude of reasons. The company is like an annuity. It doesn't grow or shrink. It performs a necessary function and does it well, but because its growth profile is stagnant, it's hard to get an investor to pay any kind of multiple that makes sense for the seller. Remember, investors want returns, and returns generally require accelerating growth.

Note: I am not a fan of ESOPs because I feel they create further issues down the road. As a strategic buyer, when I encounter a potential target to acquire and find out it's an ESOP, I run the other way and murmur, "Next!" under my breath. When every employee is an owner, every employee is also a seller who has to approve the transaction. It simply creates way too many hurdles. I could spend a ton of money doing diligence and fall in love with the company only to have the majority of employees say no to the acquisition right before the closing. It's better for me to shift my focus to someone I know is a seller.

INITIAL PUBLIC OFFERINGS

A last big exit potential that people hear about is an initial public offering (IPO). IPOs don't really make sense unless the company has at least $100 to $500 million in revenue because small public stock offerings are generally thinly traded and have high complexity and expenses due to accounting and compliance constraints. Plus, they are a pain!

In my humble opinion, I don't think a company should consider an IPO until it approaches $1 billion in revenue. I'd rather stay private and become a platform for a financial buyer or part of a large strategic company that may already be public rather than go the IPO route.

Sometimes sellers of companies will do a dual-path exit. Typically, that means they will start the process to go public while simultaneously launching a process with financial and strategic buyers. In essence, they are sailing down two paths, and they decide on the one that yields the best outcome prior to closing.

There are hundreds of books on IPOs that you can look into if you're interested. I'm here to educate you on the most common types of buyers and what a typical sales process looks like in the lower middle market to mainstream middle market, which is typically below the size required for a successful IPO. If your team of professional advisors suggests an IPO, you will need to further explore it outside the confines of this book.

SPECIAL PURPOSE ACQUISITION COMPANY (SPAC)

There is a lot of media coverage around SPACs lately. In 2020 alone, 219 SPACs were created and raised a combined $73 billion in capital. So it's a timely development in any discussion of IPOs. Although only 439 SPACs exist at the time of writing and the likelihood of you encountering a SPAC as a potential buyer is pretty slim, they are becoming more common.

Why are SPACs all the rage?

Going public through an IPO is a time-consuming hassle with no guarantee of success. Many external factors, such as recessions or pandemics, can alter the outcome, and the timing of these events cannot be controlled. Although the IPO world is unpredictable, SPACs seemingly enjoy renewed enthusiasm.

What is a SPAC?

Instead of a company going public directly, they create a shell company that raises capital in the public markets by selling stock and then seeks a company to buy. Because the shell doesn't do anything, taking it public is an easier and less time-consuming proposition. For investors, I liken a SPAC to a giant box of Cracker Jacks. Just like you have to eat the Cracker Jacks to get to the prize at the bottom, John Q Public has to invest in a SPAC without knowing what company the SPAC will eventually buy. It's not my cup of tea, but lately it seems everyone wants to play in the SPAC market. So if a SPAC comes calling, the advisory team we assemble in Part Three can help you evaluate if it is a viable exit path for your situation. Ultimately, a SPAC is just a combination of the strategic and financial buyer universes.

WHEN DO YOU CONSIDER AN ALTERNATIVE BUYER?

Although the vast majority of deals I see involve either strategic or financial buyers, we touched on several types of alternative exit strategies in this chapter. Suffice it to say that alternative buyers or exit strategies are usually driven by specific needs. Owner-operators fill niche needs like medical practices, professional services, and so on. MLBOs seem to fit best when employees or next generations take over for founders planning to retire. IPOs seem to fit really big companies, and ESOPs fit those that are hard to sell or are being gifted by a founder to their respective employees.

The team of advisors you build in Part Three will help chart the right course for your given set of circumstances.

WHAT IS YOUR POST-CLOSE FUTURE WITH AN ALTERNATIVE BUYER?

In most owner-operated, MLBO, ESOP, and search fund exits, you will exit stage left while a new owner enters from stage right. It is fairly common to have a consulting agreement for a period of time to help the buyer be successful. This is common sense for the buyer, and it often serves as an insurance policy for the seller if you are holding back a note or providing seller financing. You want to ensure the buyer succeeds so they can keep paying you! It's also common for the buyer to offer continuing office space to the seller for some amount of time. When Mike and I bought the insurance agency, we allowed the seller to keep an office for years. Emeritus title and a presence also help calm customers and any employees who are also transitioning their relationships from one owner to another.

IPOs and SPACs are a mixed bag. In these scenarios, the seller can stay on in any number of different capacities from full-time employee to CEO to non-employee chair and anywhere in between. Remember that there is typically a mandated lockup period immediately following an IPO, during which large shareholders cannot dump their stock. This helps ensure the public has time to assimilate the company's transition from private to public before the founder can cash out their chips and ride off into the sunset.

As we have learned already, multiple paths exist, and often multiple paths work, but generally it's easy to find the best exit path once you have good professional advice helping you evaluate your individual needs.

KEY TAKEAWAYS

- Owner-operators as buyers have a definite place for consideration, especially if you own a small professional or service business. They allow someone to purchase your company and transition into the driver's seat while you slide out the passenger door.

- Be on the lookout for newer hybrid approaches like search funds that may also provide attractive potential exit points.

- MLBOs, ESOPs, and IPOs are also potential exit paths. I don't focus too much on them, but your financial advisor should consider these alternate exit paths and help you determine if they are in your best interest to pursue.

PART ONE WRAP-UP

Below is a chart with some common seller circumstances and my personal opinion about who might be the right buyer. Let's be real: there are way too many nuances here for this to be your sole decision matrix. Think of this chart as your "Sell-Smart-Chart" that might be fun to consider as you continue into the next part.

CIRCUMSTANCE	STRATEGIC LIGHTS ON	STRATEGIC LIGHTS OFF	FINANCIAL	ALTERNATIVE
I want to stay working	Yes	No	Yes	IPO, SPAC
I want to retire soon	Maybe	Yes	Maybe	Any
I want top dollar	Yes	Yes	Maybe	Maybe
I am concerned about employees	Yes	No	Yes	Any
I can't find a buyer	No	No	No	ESOP
I want to roll over a portion of sale	Yes	Maybe	Yes	IPO
I want some consulting income	Yes	Yes	Yes	MLBO, IPO, owner-operator
I want a lease on my real estate	Yes	Maybe	Yes	Any
I want to limit trailing liabilities	Maybe	Maybe	Yes	Maybe

There are also some nuances when it comes to the size of your company. Nothing is hard and fast, but here are a few thoughts related to size.

VERY SMALL COMPANIES WITH GROSS EARNINGS UNDER $1 MILLION

Search for a strategic buyer purchasing several companies in the same industry to put them together or an owner-operator who wishes to take over the business. Financial buyers are few and far between at this size. The sales process for this size of company will be narrower than that described in Part Four. The same steps will often take place, but the potential buyers list will most likely be shorter or worked one at a time.

A COMPANY WITH GROSS EARNINGS IN THE $2 TO $6 MILLION RANGE

This can break either way. If you sell to a financial buyer, it will most likely be a small private equity firm with somewhat limited resources hoping to make you a platform company. It can still be very successful, but it could be tougher executing on any mergers or acquisitions that require additional financing. They won't bring in a management team, and you will follow a path very similar to what I described in Part Four of *The Private Equity Playbook*.

The other option is to choose a larger strategic company as your buyer. They have a lot of resources and a larger operation that you can learn from. The financial buyer gives you a bit more autonomy than the strategic, while the strategic's size and scale diversifies risk. There's no right or wrong. Your situational needs and your advisors will help guide you.

A COMPANY WITH GROSS EARNINGS IN THE $7 TO $40 MILLION RANGE

The best outcome is most likely a financial buyer. This size of company is broadly sought by a multitude of private equity firms, so competition has a more pronounced impact on exit value. As you get to this size, you enter the mainstream of lower middle market activity. A sale process at this size can be broad and have many suitors eager to learn more.

A VERY LARGE COMPANY WITH GROSS EARNINGS IN THE $40 TO $100-PLUS MILLION RANGE

These companies are back to having a choice. They are attractive to both large financial buyers and large strategic buyers. The question is, does the buyer plan to turn the lights off, or do you want to stay? If you want to stay, don't go with a strategic buyer that will turn the lights off on you.

FINAL WORD

No matter what buyer type you choose, never forget that if you are selling your company and staying, you will be ceding control to a new majority shareholder, and that means you'll have a new boss. Having a boss isn't necessarily a bad thing, but it is different, so be mentally prepared!

PART TWO

PREPPING YOUR BUSINESS TO SELL

Do you know the right time to start thinking about selling your business?

It's not when you're sixty-five years old and ready to retire!

In a perfect world, you started your business with the plan of one day selling it. Unfortunately, that's not how most business owners start.

I promise it's not too late. Ideally, however, you will begin prepping for sale approximately three years prior to actually transacting. Can you do it in six months? Sure. It's done all the time. But three years is the ideal time frame to make meaningful adjustments to the way the business is operated and accounted for. The earlier you can "build to sell" and align your business practices with buyer needs and expectations, the faster and smoother the process will go and the better the outcome will be.

In this section, we're going to build on the universe of buyers and start to align our thinking with their needs. We'll dive into elements of the business that you need to think about as an entrepreneur approaching this transition time in your life and your company's history. You will delve into your financial records and reporting so that you can clean up any "bad habits" you've implemented over the years. You will also address any real estate owned and look at aligning your operations.

This will ultimately lead to a smooth process, a fast close, and maximum value!

CHAPTER FOUR

↓

FINANCIAL REPORTING

It's time to take a closer look at your accounting methodologies and financial reporting practices. The universe of
buyers will spend a great deal of time scrutinizing three
years' worth of information in order to nail down and verify
your true financial picture during the diligence phase of the
transaction (discussed in Part Four).

Invariably, the entrepreneur's business expenses tend to get
merged with some level of personal expenses. Perhaps the
business now funds part of a vacation rental, or somehow
the lake house became a business expense because you let
some customers or suppliers use it once in a while. Maybe
you purchased an airplane and write off some portion of
your personal travel to the business because as you know,
every trip becomes a business trip! Perhaps Uncle Jimmy

is still on payroll even though he hasn't been active in the business for several years.

As an entrepreneur, your ultimate goal is to show as little cash profit as possible, recognize as much expense as possible, and defer recognizing revenue as long as possible—all in order to pay less taxes. Not to worry—these are all common practices in founder-owned businesses, and the universe of buyers knows this in advance.

However, a buyer's biggest need is to get a clear understanding of the business's financial picture. It can take a while to ferret through three years' worth of financial statements and tax returns. Having this kind of noise in the numbers prolongs diligence and can cause a sale process to take longer, so it's in your best interest to clean this up in advance. This doesn't mean your goal changes in terms of cash earnings and taxation. What I'm talking about here is identifying these areas and tracking them in detail. They become important when we normalize and adjust EBITDA to get credit in a sale process.

EBITDA

Those of you who read *The Private Equity Playbook* know all about EBITDA. But for those of you who are starting the journey here, let's talk a bit about this term.

Buyers will look at your cash flow but not your cash profit. Some companies have debt to service. Others are busy investing in technology or opening new offices and growing. Cash profits can vary wildly among businesses in the same industry, and as a result, they often don't provide a clear picture with respect to the health or true value of a business. One business may not be investing in itself or its future, so it may have a higher cash profit than a business on a fast growth trajectory doing the right things for its future. A company with less cash profit may actually be more valuable to a buyer because it is growing as compared to a company that is not investing for its future, has deferred expenses, and is stagnant.

In order to normalize valuation, the universe of buyers we discussed in Part One will be focusing on EBITDA (pronounced as three syllables: e-bit-dah), which stands for "earnings before interest, taxes, depreciation, and amortization" and is a line on the financial statement you may not have heard of before.

This number serves to level the valuation playing field when compared to other companies in the same industry, and it is a measure by which all companies are valued by most strategic and financial buyers.

There are different types of EBITDA.

AS-REPORTED EBITDA

As-reported EBITDA, or definitional EBITDA, is based solely on what happened for the financial period (month, quarter, year) as reported by the numbers submitted on your financial statements. In essence, it only considers the literal definitional adjustments to net income to derive at EBITDA. You might say that reported EBITDA is simply "whatever it is."

ADJUSTED EBITDA

As-reported EBITDA is frequently adjusted when providing financial statements to prospective buyers or lenders. These adjustments are added back to the reported EBITDA to create your adjusted EBITDA. Several types of adjustments can be made:

Extraordinary Expenses

These are one-time expenses that won't reoccur in the future. Perhaps you restructured a department and had layoffs. Because you're a generous person, let's say you paid a large severance to the employees who were displaced by that fancy new piece of software. Those severance expenses impacted your EBITDA for a given time period, but you wouldn't have those expenses the next year. As a result, you would seek to get credit for those expenses from a buyer by adding them back to earnings.

Normalizing Adjustments

An example of normalizing adjustments would be layering in rent expense if the company doesn't pay rent today. For example, maybe the owner owns the building and doesn't charge the company rent, but the buyer of the business isn't buying the building and will now need to start paying market rent.

Out-of-Period Adjustments

These adjustments are made when income or expenses were recorded in the incorrect month or year and needs to be moved to the appropriate period. An example of this would be a bonus expense that is recorded all at year-end (or even after year-end) but should be expensed throughout the year (or moved to the appropriate year).

PRO FORMA ADJUSTED EBITDA

Pro forma adjusted EBITDA, sometimes called run rate EBITDA, takes those adjustments and adds another layer of projections on top. Sometimes there are seller pro forma adjustments (changes the seller has made or anticipates making) and buyer pro forma adjustments (changes the buyer is planning to make).

These adjustments tend to be more subjective in nature. Examples might include a seller thinking they will be moving from one office to another at a reduced rent, or a buyer thinking they will need to add a controller to shore up a weak accounting department. These adjustments cut both ways and may be in various stages of execution.

During the course of the year, things happen. Perhaps you signed three big new accounts, one three months into the year, another six months into the year, and the last one eleven months into the year. In your as-reported EBITDA for that period, there are only nine months of revenue from the first contract, six months from the second, and one month from the third. In the next year, there will be twelve months of revenue from all three of those contracts, so your business could state a pro forma EBITDA where you project forward the revenue impact of that new business over the next twelve months.

Anytime you pro forma positive gains, you need to pro forma losses too. Maybe you lost a contract eight months into the year. Next year, you will have no revenue from that customer, so you'll need to remove those eight months going forward in a pro forma calculation. Don't forget those losses. Maybe rent goes up next year. Payroll costs go up 3 percent after you give raises. The more accurate you are when making these adjustments, the faster you'll get through a sale process. Your buyer will do the work to catch one-sided adjustments, so save yourself both time by being accurate.

In general, inside a growing company, as-reported EBITDA

will be lower than adjusted EBITDA, and adjusted EBITDA will be lower than pro forma adjusted EBITDA. The seller's goal is to adjust the EBITDA and project forward based on business signed and business lost, expenses that don't survive the sale, and so forth.

Note: In today's world, with a lot of financial buyers and strategic buyers out looking for companies to buy, sellers are getting incredibly aggressive at pumping up their reported EBITDA by using a multitude of adjustments—some legitimate to add back and others not. If I'm buying a company with $2 million in EBITDA and 50 percent of those earnings are add-backs, you can bet your life I'm going to scrutinize those adjustments very carefully when conducting financial diligence. I'll give a seller credit for real ones, but I'll discount the ones that I think cross a line into the realm of fantasy. In my world, we call that kind of fantasy "mixing Kool-Aid" because the seller wants me to "drink their Kool-Aid." As a buyer, I need to resist.

OTHER TYPES OF EBITDA

There are many other related EBITDA terms including trailing twelve months (TTM) EBITDA, TTM adjusted EBITDA, and TTM pro forma adjusted EBITDA. You'll hear many different flavors and versions used differently. How people define EBITDA can vary pretty wildly too. As a result, it's always good to lay a foundation with your accountant and the universe of buyers so everyone is on a level playing field.

Items I included in adjusted EBITDA in this book may be another person's pro forma adjusted EBITDA. There's no right or wrong. I'm not an accountant, nor do I pretend to be one. And when I ask accountants or read investment guides, I never get uniform answers. Everyone agrees what EBITDA is. When you add words or acronyms in front of the term, the water gets a little murky.

The way I like to think about it is this: As-reported or plain old EBITDA is what it is. Adjusted EBITDA adds back one-time anomalies that occurred in the period, and pro forma adjusted EBITDA includes any forward-looking projections.

EBITDA is a game, and how well you understand and play it will have a direct impact on the purchase price you receive when selling your business. Presenting buyers with these numbers early in the process adds credibility in your quest for maximum value. You'll be seen as a sophisticated seller who shouldn't be toyed with.

Note: Buyers will want to see three years of financial statements. You don't need to alter habits. Your goal until you sell remains to pay as little taxes as possible. But the sophistication of your reporting needs to change in order for you to get credit for proper adjustments and obtain maximum value.

CASH-BASED ACCOUNTING VERSUS ACCRUAL-BASED ACCOUNTING

Now that you know a little about EBITDA, let's look at the different methods of accounting.

Cash-based accounting is exactly that. You recognize revenue when the money comes in, and you recognize expenses when you write a check. Cash-based accounting makes life easy for many small to medium-sized businesses. When you are built to not pay taxes, it's an easy methodology to follow and requires less effort from you, your accounting team, and your tax preparer. For some companies, regardless of size, it's always a good choice.

For others, it can be problematic in a sale because revenue and earnings may swing wildly from period to period based solely on when transactions take place and when entries are made into the accounting system. For these companies, accrual-based accounting is a better strategy, and if done in advance, it will make a sale process go faster and smoother.

Let's consider a company with twenty-five employees on an annual bonus plan. In a cash accounting method, you'd recognize the expense of paying those annual bonuses in the month you paid them. If each employee earned $4,800, you'd have $120,000 in expenses go against earnings in one month. In an accrual-based accounting system, you would accrue $10,000 each month in expenses rather than taking a $120,000 hit in one month.

In this type of system, cash flows are separated from reporting. You still need to pay that cash all at one time when you pay bonuses, but it distributes revenue and expenses across a year of financial statements.

It's easier to determine if a business is growing, stagnating, or declining if you view their accrual-based accounting. Cash-based accounting is generally fine for small businesses, but at some point, as you grow, your level of business sophistication needs to grow along with you.

There is no right or wrong, but generally speaking, a buyer will spend a great deal of time studying your financials and building an investment model based on how the business performs over time. The more your financial statements are in order, the faster and smoother a sale process will go, regardless of which accounting methodology you are using.

GAAP

GAAP (pronounced as one syllable, "gap") stands for "generally accepted accounting practices." It's the set of rules that all CPAs use to prepare financial statements for a company. GAAP informs and lays the ground rules for how a business is audited. The universe of buyers needs to get very comfortable with the financial reporting of the company they are considering buying. Better books and more standardized rules means more reliable numbers, which are faster and easier to verify. GAAP accounting practices are mandatory in a public company, but non-GAAP is acceptable in private companies. The closer you are to GAAP, the easier it is for sophisticated buyers to do their work and get comfortable with your financial statements.

Purchase offers and bids for companies typically made represent some multiple of EBITDA. The easier it is for a buyer to attain comfort level on your EBITDA and how consistent your business has performed over time, the faster the sale process and the higher the bids.

For the current industry I purchase for, it is typical for me to pay five to six times EBITDA. So if a company has an accepted pro forma adjusted EBITDA of $2 million and I'm paying five times EBITDA, I will make a bid of $10 million for that business. If I really like the business, it's clean, and it's doing better than the average, I may bid $12 million or more.

QUALITY OF EARNINGS

A buyer's job in diligence is to do what accountants call a *quality of earnings* report, or Q of E. A buy-side Q of E is the document that buyers use to verify your EBITDA, evaluate how it has performed over time, project where it will be in the future, and inform their thinking on what bid to offer for a business. Buyers may perform the Q of E internally or use a third-party firm that specializes in transactional diligence.

Although all buyers do a Q of E on your business, you shouldn't be sitting around in the dark wondering what their offer will be when their work is done. You should already know what the buyer's report will say because you should have already done a sell-side Q of E before you put the company up for sale.

Q of E calculations are done by humans, and like EBITDA, they can get a little muddled. Because of this, sophisticated sellers want to give potential buyers their version first. They will even offer up time with their preparer so buyers can cut to the chase and understand how the seller got the number they did. This is where you can presell a buyer on that Kool-Aid we talked about earlier.

From a financial perspective, it's important to start understanding and cleaning up your own accounting practices. A potential seller who really has their act together should talk to their accountant about having them do an independent sell-side Q of E and prepare annual audited financial statements.

CHANGE THE CONVERSATION

Potential buyers want to see at least three years' worth of

financial statements on the business. They want to know if the business is growing, shrinking, or treading water. Are earnings increasing? Is top-line revenue increasing? They want to understand as much as possible about your business.

Doing this work in advance changes the conversation. If someone comes knocking on your door and expresses interest in your company and you hand them a shoebox filled with receipts and three years' worth of files from your computer system, they will have to do all the work to normalize your finances and create a Q of E. They will then come back to you with what they believe is an applicable purchase price.

But if you want to know ahead of time what to expect and the potential value of your business, you'll need to spend time and money to determine these numbers. Armed with that information, you will be a sophisticated seller, and buyers will know they need to be mindful of how they proceed. It also shifts the dynamic of how the buyer thinks about the business. It changes their fear of "I have to try to create this" to "This is beautiful! They already have it. This is a business I want to own." Good financials, audited financial statements, and sell-side Q of E are all important to driving *maximum value*.

EXPECTATIONS BASED ON SIZE

When it comes to your financial reporting, size matters, and the universe of buyers has a different set of expectations based on the size of company they seek to purchase. The larger a company, the more likely they are to use GAAP and accrual-based accounting. They likely have an outside audit firm that helps them prepare their financial statements and taxes and develop a sell-side Q of E.

If you're a small business with $1 million in earnings or less, it's okay to have QuickBooks files and an accountant who helps you create your as-reported, adjusted, and pro forma adjusted EBITDA for a three-year period.

Everyone, regardless of size, needs to:

- Have an awareness of their financial reporting.
- Understand the term "EBITDA."
- Understand if their revenue is growing, stagnant, or declining.
- Understand if earnings are growing, stagnant, or declining.
- Be able to tell the story about the business with some level of sophistication.

KEY TAKEAWAYS

- The cleaner your books, the faster the sale process.

- Understanding your own EBITDA helps make you a more knowl-edgeable seller.

- Doing your own sell-side Q of E changes the conversation.

- Consider having your CPA start doing audited financial state-ments now.

CHAPTER FIVE

REAL ESTATE

Most entrepreneurs I have encountered in my career tend to be on the conservative side and like to own their own buildings. Over the past twenty years, I've bought more than fifty companies, and in nearly every case—at least 90 percent or more—the company has owned real estate.

These aren't startups, obviously. On day one, a business owner may work out of their home, their truck, or a rented space. But if you build an empire over decades, chances are you own multiple pieces of real estate.

This is typical. Many people want to control their expenses. WASH, for example, was founded in the 1940s by a husband and wife who grew up during the Great Depression and World War II when things were rationed and heavily controlled. Like most people who grew up in that era, they had a deeply ingrained mindset that renting things or having debt wasn't good. Over the decades, every time they opened a new office, they bought the real estate that housed it. Fifty years down the road, they had amassed a massive real estate footprint worth hundreds of millions of dollars. I was hired to be the first person outside the family to run the business, and I saw this portfolio of owned properties up close and personal.

Here's the thing. No buyer—strategic or financial—wants to own your real estate!

REAL ESTATE IS TOO LONG TERM OF AN INVESTMENT

Nearly 50 percent of all companies sold today will be sold to a private equity buyout fund. The focus of a private equity buyout fund is to acquire established companies with real revenue and a track record of being in business over an extended period of time.

Private equity funds tend to have a ten-year maturity and a typical hold period of five years on the companies they buy. Real estate is considered a very long-term investment and thus is not capital efficient when private equity seeks to generate three times the return on its money over a five-year period of time. Real estate can trend down or up, but you can't typically complete a full real estate cycle during the hold period of private equity.

That's not to say that there are not specialty funds in private equity whose sole purpose is to make real estate investments. If you are in the business of owning and managing real estate, then your universe of potential suitors includes specialty funds as financial buyers.

For the rest of you, your financial buyer comes from private equity buyout funds. If you're an entrepreneur who has a portion of your net worth tied up in real estate, know that the private equity firm or strategic buyer has zero interest in owning the real estate.

REAL ESTATE IS A DIFFERENT ASSET CLASS

Real estate is also in a different asset class from a company. When a buyer purchases a company and by happenstance obtains their real estate, this not only mixes asset classes but also requires a completely different set of diligence requirements. Do they like the company? Do they also like all the real estate? Those answers may differ, and it's simply a bridge that's way too far and hard for any buyer to cross.

EXTRACT REAL ESTATE TO A NEW ENTITY

Real estate issues should be addressed one to three years before you sell because you may need to spin out your real estate into a separate entity. In doing this, you create a

second empire that was built as a part of your first empire—
the one you intend to sell.

After you spin the real estate out of the business, you need
to put in place a fair market lease between your business
and the real estate. In essence, you'll become your own
landlord. Meet with your advisory team (discussed in Part
Three) to discuss the pros and cons of how you structure that
real estate deal. There are tax-efficient and non-tax-efficient
methods, and each situation is different.

*Note: Remember when we discussed EBITDA adjustments? If
you owned your real estate and were not charging the company
a fair market rent for the space, you'll need to now make an
adjustment to reflect that the ongoing business will have rent
payments to make on its buildings. Not charging rent may have
artificially increased your EBITDA.*

CREATE AN ONGOING INCOME STREAM

When you sell your company, your ongoing income stream
may include lease payments from the company for rent.
Moving is expensive and a hassle. Provided you have a reasonable fair-market lease with a duration of five to seven
years, chances are that the new owner will continue that
lease for some period of time. Don't play games, though. If
a buyer sees an above-market rent for a term that far exceeds
market norms, they will make you accept a cancellation or

renegotiation of terms as a condition of sale. I have seen some sellers try to get twenty-year lease terms on buildings. That's nice if you can get it—but not when I'm your buyer!

The company I discussed earlier, WASH, ended up owning hundreds of millions of dollars of commercial real estate. They created a second company, and even though they sold WASH over thirteen years ago, they still own a portfolio of properties to this day. Now they are in the business of real estate!

In addition, after the sale took place and the family no longer owned the company, because I had fair-market rents in place, they continued to generate income on the properties the company occupied for several years into the future. As we vacated properties due to shifting needs, they would either continue to own the buildings with new tenants or sell them and use the proceeds for other real estate-related investments.

It's not bad to own real estate as an entrepreneur. The key is to understand the impacts on the sale and how you can continue to own and even generate new income.

By understanding this now, you're in a much better position to spin the real estate off into a second entity and set up a lease. The last thing you want to do is be in the middle of a sale and have to establish these elements.

KEY TAKEAWAYS

- No buyer wants your real estate.

- If you carve it out ahead of time, the sale will go faster.

- True market lease terms let you put in place an income-generating lease if your plan is to be a landlord.

CHAPTER SIX

↓

ALIGNING OPERATIONS

As you go through the sales process, you'll be developing a story for the universe of potential buyers. The first part of the narrative is whether you plan to stay or leave. If you're leaving, who will take over? How will you make sure that business will continue as normal? Are the revenue and growth sustainable in your absence? Even if you're staying, a buyer will want to know your plans to accelerate growth during the hold period (if a financial buyer) and what strategic gaps you'll help fill (if a strategic buyer).

They'll want to know how you'll grow organically and how you can improve margins on your existing business. Is there space to invest in technology and software to be more efficient and thus more profitable? Can you scale your business?

The goal for a new owner is to grow your business faster,

and this story needs to be well orchestrated. Here is how you will answer these questions and align your operations now to meet their goals.

WILL YOU STAY OR WILL YOU GO?

As you shift into the sales process, it's important to understand your personal goals for the future.

If you're in your mid-forties or mid-fifties, you probably don't intend to retire, so you will most likely be looking for a financial buyer or a strategic buyer that does not plan to turn the lights off so you can continue working in the business. What drives you to sell is a desire to diversify your empire and create a protected hedge for retirement. Very few entrepreneurs I have encountered know how to retire!

If you are older and don't want to continue running the business, you might be looking for a path out. Over the course of my career, I've learned that no matter how much money I make, I can't buy time. It's the one element that is critical but can't be purchased. But just because you're ready to retire doesn't mean you need to leave the business altogether. You can become a rollover investor and get a second bite of the apple, a consultant, a part-time employee—many options exist with a potential new owner.

Most financial buyers of a business aren't buying the business—they are investing in *you*. They are buying your relationships. They're buying all the hard work you put into your business over the last two or three decades, and unless they are a strategic buyer looking to turn the lights off, they really don't want you to ride off into the sunset.

They fear what happens if you walk out the door. Will the clients stay? Will the revenues remain? Will the earnings they are paying a multiple on still exist? Will the employees stay? They are most fearful that the business they are buying is a house of cards and when you exit and close the door, the wind will knock it all down into a pile of rubble.

SUCCESSION PLANNING AND TEAM DEVELOPMENT

A lot of entrepreneurs are strong-willed. There's no place in their organization for a strong number two, and they haven't really developed someone to succeed them in the business.

But it's no longer me versus we.

If you plan to retire, you need to start thinking about succession planning and team development. If there's nobody to stay on—a family member or a strong second person—a buyer will view this as a large risk. Buyers don't like risks! They want to purchase a sure thing. So it's important to spend time thinking about the story you're going to tell. It doesn't matter if the buyer is strategic or financial—your story needs to be about long-term growth. You need to be able to discuss the sustainability of the business and its revenue streams, even if you depart.

Take time to build a strong number two in your organization. Rather than seeing them as a potential threat or competition, you need to see this person as your golden ticket into retirement. The goal is to build up a leadership team that will protect the business, relationships, and continued growth.

WHAT IS YOUR ORGANIC (AND INORGANIC) GROWTH TRAJECTORY?

The next part of your story is the growth trajectory of your business. If you already read *The Private Equity Playbook*, you understand the basic levers of growth:

LEVER ONE: ORGANIC GROWTH

- Increase price.
- Increase volume.

LEVER TWO: MARGIN EXPANSION

- Lower the cost of servicing your existing revenue via:
  ◦ Process improvement.
  ◦ Investing in technology.

LEVER THREE: BUY AND BUILD

- Acquire companies to:
  - Accelerate growth.
  - Build density.
  - Enter new markets.
  - Add capability.
- Harness multiple arbitrages to pay lower multiples than you ultimately will sell for later.

LEVER FOUR: WORK WITH CONSULTANTS

- Add surge capacity.
- Leverage best-practice sharing from other engagements.
- Add generic expertise you may not have.

Those levers are the same with a financial buyer or a strategic buyer backed by private equity. You will need to present the business as it stands today and the potential growth. "We've been growing at an average of X percent, and earnings have been growing at Y percent. As I look at the next five years, if I had a partner and additional capital, here is how I could accelerate that growth, bend the curve, and attain new heights. I could expand into new markets, add this product line, etc."

In case you are curious about the magnitude we are talking about, I did some research on the companies I have run over the past twenty years. On average, prior to my arrival, the companies had a compounded annual growth rate, or CAGR (pronounced as two syllables, "kay-grr"), that ranged from 2 to 8 percent. In all cases, I was able to take those existing businesses and bend the growth curve to achieve CAGR of 24 to 27 percent. If you have a financial buyer, this is the level of increase required to generate the outsized returns that private equity is known for. How are you going to do that? In my career running mature B2B service companies, that equates to getting organic growth into the high single digits, adding in a few points of margin improvement, and then using buy and build as the central growth strategy to punch it up to the high 20s. If you are lucky enough to be growing organically at a sustained rate in the high 20s, your story will be dramatically different from mine.

Buyers want to know your past because that informs historical growth rates and stability. They also want to know about your future. All buyers are paying a market rate for your company, and in order to get an outsized return on investment, they will need to figure out how to accelerate your growth. Build a story around those levers of growth that will get them excited so they potentially pay more for your business than they would for someone who has no idea of their needs or growth plans. A company that grows by 10 percent a year doubles in size in seven years—that's far too long! At CoolSys, we doubled revenue and tripled EBITDA in twenty-seven months.

If you'd like to read more about the process of connecting *Talent to Value™* to achieve outsized growth rates of the magnitude we are talking about here, I'd encourage you to read books by my friend and mentor Sandy Ogg, founder of CEO.works. Sandy is a pioneer in helping companies identify their key value drivers (work to be done) and connecting them to the key individuals who will own making it happen. Sandy has spent a lifetime perfecting his methodology at places like Motorola, Unilever, and Blackstone and has been a big influencer on how I think about accelerating growth in a company.

ARE THERE MERGER AND ACQUISITION OPPORTUNITIES?

If you think your company will be acquired as part of a mergers-and-acquisitions strategy, it is worthwhile to think about other companies that could supplement yours. Document those you could potentially purchase if you had capital from an additional source. This all goes back to the conversation we had in Part One. Do you want to be a platform company for a financial buyer, or do you want to be purchased by a strategic buyer and become part of a larger collective?

As a platform company, you're the base a financial buyer will use to grow, so it's key that you identify companies that are similar to yours. "Here are five companies. I know some of the owners, and these are potential businesses to purchase after you buy my company. We could double or triple the size of the company in three years."

CAN YOUR BUSINESS SCALE WITH EFFICIENCY?

If your buyer is a financial firm, one of the keys to accelerating growth is building a platform that can scale with efficiency. This is accomplished with process simplicity and repeatability coupled with technology. Think about the software platforms you run the business on today. If the company doubled or tripled in size, could your existing systems handle the increased volume? Where are the bottlenecks and choke points that slow you down today? Identifying and developing a plan for addressing them will help your buyer gain confidence.

If your buyer is strategic, hopefully they will bring their systems to you. Be inquisitive and show some enthusiasm about the potential for change. Be willing to engage in discovery around ways the strategic buyer can help you gain a more efficient and scalable platform from which to grow. You may not realize this, but in fact, everything you say and do—your facial expressions, attitude, and enthusiasm—is being cataloged by the buyer universe. The more you demonstrate passion for your business and an openness to truly partner, the more points you put on the scoreboard with them, and the more likely it is that you'll achieve maximum value.

HOW DOES YOUR BUSINESS PERFORM DURING RECESSIONS/PANDEMICS?

Most buyers will spend a lot of time and effort during diligence to become educated on your business. If you were in business in 2008–2009 (the Great Recession), they will absolutely want to know how you performed during the recession. After 2020, they will want to know how you performed during the pandemic.

Prior to the pandemic, we were in a golden bull market that had extended for many years. Stock prices had been climbing for several years, and everyone knew a recession was on the horizon. Because of these cycles, buyers want to understand how your business performed in the last recession, whenever that may have been. They will want to know:

- What happened to your revenue?
- How far did it decline?
- Did you do well during that time frame?
- Were you hit hard, or did you grow during this time?

These elements are important because everyone is concerned about the next recession, and the buyer universe wants to understand the risks of buying your business.

After the pandemic, buyers will likely ask how your business was hit:

- Were you an essential business?
- What happened to revenue?
- What happened to your customer base?

- What happened to your expenses?
- Did you lay off employees?
- Did you hire new employees and grow?

When I ran WASH, we managed 77,000 common-area laundry rooms spread across apartment complexes, colleges, military bases, and so forth in North America for residents who didn't have washer/dryer units inside the residential units. We signed contracts and long-term leases and shared the revenue with the apartment owners and complex managers.

During the Great Recession, we learned several things about commercial laundry operations. We learned that even in a recession, people still need to do laundry. It didn't matter if they were employed or unemployed. Laundry still had some resilience.

However, we learned that unemployed people don't do as much laundry as employed people. For example, California had a building boom in the housing market before the Great Recession, but in 2008, construction ground to a halt. A lot of workers in construction and related businesses were laid off. Although they collected unemployment, they weren't getting as dirty sitting at their homes, so they did less laundry.

This type of story is what a buyer wants to hear. You need to understand how your business performed during the last big recession and during the global pandemic. If your business is recession-proof or recession-resistant, pandemic-proof or pandemic-resistant, you will ultimately be worth more money than a company that is not. Your company will have a higher value than one that was not essential and took a massive hit to earnings.

You want to be ready for these types of questions and understand the direct impact on the valuation. Understand the positive aspects, even if you were hit hard. Let's say you own a service company, and your primary focus and customer is the restaurant and retail area. You likely got hammered hard in the pandemic, but in five years, you might recover and be doing well. Your story might look like this: "During the global pandemic, I was heavily reliant on nonessential businesses. Over the last five years, I strategically made a shift to focus on finding new customers that are essential businesses. As a result, my revenue has grown. If another pandemic started tomorrow, I would not be impacted as much as I was the first time." The goal isn't to just abandon your business. You love the restaurant industry. But how can you make it more pandemic-proof? If there is a lockdown, what is your plan? How do you create new revenue streams that are resilient yet still allow you to stay in your core business?

This information is important to any type of buyer, strategic or financial. They want to know how you did during the pandemic, any business habits you've altered, and the types of products and services you could provide during times of concern.

By knowing this information up front and being able to present it quickly and accurately, you show that you are an educated seller. The buyer will recognize that you are very thoughtful about your business, and you will likely get a higher valuation than another seller who has not done this work.

PEAK TO TROUGH

This may be brought up during the sales process: "Hey, how did you perform during the last recession? What was your peak to trough?" The peak is your revenue before the recession hit. Your trough is how far you fell. Then there is the length of time to recover back to your peak. So you may say you fell 10 percent and your length of recovery was eighteen months. The lower your peak to trough and the shorter your recovery time, the better a buyer views the valuation. This is especially true for a private equity investor because a recession can hit at any time. They don't plan to hold your business for a long time, so the faster your recovery, the more valuable you are in that instance. They are willing to pay extra for a company that will do well for their short-term investment horizon.

THE BUSINESS MUST SURVIVE AND THRIVE

The story you present is critical to a buyer because they want to see how your business will survive and thrive. Whether you stay or go, whether you are hit by a truck or win the lottery, how will the business survive?

When you align your thinking with the buyer's needs, you'll be far better prepared to handle an actual emergency, and you'll be valued higher by those financial or strategic buyers.

Ideally, you will start this process at least a few years before you plan to sell so you can make strategic changes and see the impact on your business. Sure, you could prepare a business to sell in six months. But ideally, you will have adequate time to modify operations, habits, and business practices prior to selling in order to attract the buyer universe that is willing to pay maximum value. Remember, this book isn't about selling fast—it's about selling smart to achieve maximum value.

If you're the restaurant owner above and learned that during the global pandemic that you would be closed to anyone other than takeout customers, what can you do differently so you are better prepared three years from now? Well, who stayed open? Grocery stores were open. Delis were open. Perhaps you could begin developing a line of prepackaged foods as a new distribution method. Perhaps you could deliver meals to homeless shelters, Meals on Wheels, and older people who are sheltered at home. Instead of selling a single meal, maybe you could package three meals for the next day or start a meal subscription service.

When you create these pivots for your business, you show that you are a businessperson who doesn't just ride the economic wave up and down but rather knows how to maximize revenue in up cycles and minimize the downside in economic downturns.

The key is to think strategically about how you could alter your business to be even more successful. Build a business that caters to the future universe of buyers and plays into the strengths of what they're seeking to buy. Start making those nuanced changes now. Obtain your audited financials, and begin working on your sell-side Q of E. Begin to track revenue and earnings growth. Think about operations, and build a strong leadership team. Most entrepreneurs leave money on the table because they don't put enough forethought into such matters in the years leading up to the sale.

You're not just preparing to sell; you're also running a better business because you're starting to think about items that are important to the future owners of the business. Their objective is to grow it three times larger than it currently is today, and they want to do that in a short period of time. You are helping get them there.

KEY TAKEAWAYS

- You need an heir apparent if you intend to leave after the sale.

- If you want maximum value, you need to have a growth story.

- Understanding your competitors and adding a potential buy and build story increases your valuation.

- Adapting for recessions and pandemics yields tangible increases to valuations.

PART TWO WRAP-UP

In Part Two, we focused on the key aspects of preparing your business for sale, including financial, real estate, leadership, and operational areas. These actions generally take time to accomplish, so you should start doing them in the years leading up to a sale.

I stated several times that once you enter the sales process, you will close faster and for a higher value if you are properly prepared. There is a reason I keep referencing time, so let's discuss why it is so important.

Over the course of the last four years, I've bought eighteen companies in the HVAC space. When a company has clean books and a clear understanding of their EBITDA and knows how their revenue and earnings are growing, I have been able to close a deal in as little as twenty-three days. Meanwhile, a company running on spreadsheets with absolutely no idea of their revenue or EBITDA requires me to create this information during diligence. This type of deal takes an average of six months to complete. In a worst-case scenario, it could take as long as a year.

Does time matter to you? It should. Sometimes a few days or weeks is the difference between getting a deal done and having it completely fall apart along with the markets.

Back in 2008, I was in the market to sell WASH. We closed the deal on September 10. Just a few short weeks later—September 29, to be exact—the stock market collapsed, and all deal activity died as the Great Recession of 2008 set in. Had I been caught by the recession, I would not have been able to complete the sale of the business for some time. Eventually, like all recessions, the market recovered to pre-recession norms. In this case, I would have lost a few years, but eventually I'd still have been able to sell.

Sometimes, though, companies or industries don't fully recover. In January 2020, businesses in the United States were doing fine. The stock market was at an all-time high. In March, the world turned upside down with the COVID-19 pandemic. Let's say you owned a chain of movie theaters. In January, you looked pretty good. In April, you very well may have been out of business. Had you tried to sell your business in January with a good growth story and detailed financials, you would have sold just fine. If you didn't have your documents and story all aligned, you probably wouldn't have sold. Unfortunately, the pandemic has most likely lowered the value of that industry forever. Movie theaters are nonessential businesses, and it may take a long time to get back to pre-pandemic norms—if they ever do.

When you're a seller, time is not your friend. You want to be on top of your company's financial documents and have a clear understanding of your financial picture, and you want to deal with your real estate ahead of time. You should have a leadership succession plan in place if necessary and have a clear growth story to tell the marketplace. The stock market can crash. A pandemic can send everyone into quarantine. The more you understand and the better positioned you are, the faster you can get a deal done and get the money in the bank.

That is what matters!

PART THREE

BUILD YOUR ADVISORY TEAM

You're an expert at running your business, but I bet you don't know the four people you need on your team to secure the best outcome when selling. Don't worry. I'm here to walk you through their roles and how they help you get maximum value.

I've mentioned before that I've purchased more than fifty companies in my career. The typical size is $20 to $30 million in revenue, with the largest at $125 million. These purchases occurred while I was running larger companies and executing a buy and build strategy as a platform company for private equity. All fifty of these companies were add-on acquisitions where I was a strategic buyer.

When I begin interacting with sellers and their teams of advisors, I can tell within a matter of minutes if they are competent or not. There are telltale signs, and I'm here to make sure you have the right ones when you step into the boardroom.

It is important to get competent advice from professionals who specialize in the sale of companies. This is not the time to grab your Rolodex of contacts. Yes, on the finance side, you have someone who does your taxes and helps when you need it with corporate taxes, audits, and other compliance matters. Likewise, you have someone in legal to help you with contracts and credit agreements and deal with the occasional slip and fall, wrongful termination, or other employee matter. You've used your good friend as needed for someone who's quick and available. But now you need specific, expert accounting, tax, legal, and investment banking advice.

The type of advice you need when selling a company is very different than the type of advice you needed to run your company. The people you are using today may or may not be the best resources to aid you with a sale process. It's time to take a long, hard look in the mirror and understand that you are an absolute expert at building and running your business, but you are not an expert at selling it. Check your ego at the door, and recognize that this is not something that you do every day. So you need help from competent advisors, which we will discuss here.

CHAPTER SEVEN

↓

TAX ADVISORS AND ACCOUNTANTS

Over the course of building your business, you have undoubtedly sought professional help from accountants and tax advisors. You may have started out using QuickBooks and TurboTax. But I'm sure as your business grew, there came a time when you started needing outside advice.

When you are a business owner, you can categorize the type of help you need along two lines: personal and business. On the personal side, depending on how you set up your business entity, the help includes filing your personal income tax in one or more states and your federal taxes. The more sophisticated your structure, the more you needed help with the business to make sure you filed the appropriate types of returns to local, state, and federal agencies for the business's sales, payroll, and income taxes.

When the time comes to consider selling a company, you need additional assistance. You need to understand your personal tax situation and develop your sell-side Q of E report. You also need help with accounting and financial statements. Your tax advisors and accountants will be your experts.

WHY YOU NEED A PERSONAL TAX ADVISOR

Tax advice is different from accounting advice. As an owner selling your business, you're about to receive a large windfall. You need to prepare for this large payday, and that requires very specific tax planning to receive the maximum amount after the sale.

It is important to begin preparing to sell your company years in advance. Let's say your company does business in California, Nevada, and Arizona. If you are a California resident, the sale of your company and your personal windfall is likely to incur a state income or capital gains tax in the top bracket of 13.3 percent.

Note: Top brackets and rates change, so consider this example just for illustrative purposes. In 2020, California contemplated raising the highest personal tax bracket to more than 16 percent, and for the first time in US history, the state also considered an

annual 0.4 percent wealth tax on individuals with a net worth
of over $30 million. If you are a Nevada resident, the income
tax would be zero.

If your business sells for $20 million, you're looking at a tax
burden that is millions of dollars different, depending on
your state of residency. Now imagine your business sells for
a gain of $100 million. Ouch! That's at least $13 million in
tax differential. It's no wonder we constantly see in the news
that people and companies are leaving places like California,
New York, and New Jersey for places like Texas, Nevada, and
Florida. For most business owners, big paydays don't happen
every day, so maximizing what you receive needs to be a
strong consideration in planning an exit and domiciling a
business. Remember that maximum value isn't just about
getting the highest price; it's also about being tax efficient
and retaining the maximum amount of that money.

So what can you do? Well, you might want to look at how far
out you plan to sell your business and the tax ramifications
of where you choose to call home. If you have a multistate
business, you can move and become a resident of the state
that will have a more tax-friendly treatment of the windfall
that you're going to receive. Generally speaking, the time to
move is not during the year of the sale. Most tax jurisdictions
are very aggressive when it comes to collecting the tax from
business owners or people who sell businesses and move
right before or during the sale process. They also don't take

kindly to people who try to play games. If you own homes in California and Nevada but spend all your time in California, you will get challenged and be audited, and you will lose. You can't mail it in when it comes to picking a place to live as a business owner. You need to be focused on the tax ramifications as far in advance as possible.

This is just one of many considerations that your personal tax advisor can help with—and a residency decision should probably involve your attorney (discussed in further detail in Chapter Eight) because multiple steps are needed to establish residency.

Another consideration is the structure of your company. Did you set it up as a sole proprietor, LLC, S corp, or C corp? These all affect the amount you will receive after the sale of your company, how the proceeds will be taxed, and how you determine the appropriate type of sale (stock versus asset) for your company.

WHY YOU NEED A BUSINESS TAX ADVISOR

When an entrepreneur sells a company, there are typically two types of purchase agreements or transactions that can take place: asset deals and stock deals.

If a company exists and the stock of the company is sold, that will generally result in more favorable tax treatment for the seller of the business. However, the vast majority of buyers don't want to do stock deals; rather, they want to do asset deals. Asset deals generally—but not always—result in a tax differential. Sellers should understand the specific amount of money that difference equates to; it may be important later.

The rationale is that if someone buys a company using a stock transaction, the entrepreneur walks out the back door, and the buyer is left holding all potential trailing liabilities. For example, a service business had gas pumps on the property to refill their vehicles. The business buried the gas pumps twenty years ago and stopped using them five years ago. They moved to a new location, so they are not even occupying the old property at the time of sale. A leak is detected five years after the new owner of the business buys it, and because they did a stock deal, the new owner just inherited all of these trailing liabilities. Ever heard of the term "superfund cleanup site"? I have. You don't want to!

A stock transaction also takes a lot longer because the buyer will require more in-depth diligence to discover potential trailing issues like the buried gas tanks example used above.

A seller wants to do a stock sale because of the more favorable tax treatment. Thus, as a seller, you need advice regarding the structure of the company and the preferred method of sale, and then you need to do some analysis around the differential. If it is a $200,000 benefit to you to do a stock deal, you can always increase your purchase price by $200,000 if the buyer wants an asset sale. I mention this because some buyers will refuse to do stock deals. Anyone who owns a business today already owns the trailing liabilities that might exist. It's a risk of being in business. When selling, it's nice to jettison those potential liabilities during the sale, but not all buyers are willing to assume them. If all buyers feel this way, it could be the difference between getting a deal done and not.

In addition to this type of liability, there are also other inherent liabilities around 401(k)s or pension plans. You need good advice always.

Typically, larger companies that will become platform companies for financial buyers can be sold as stock deals. To help facilitate any issues, the buyer or seller will often purchase an insurance policy to cover most trailing liabilities. These policies are expensive, require extensive diligence by the buyer, and have high deductibles. They can, however, make sure that unforeseen liabilities are not catastrophic to the buyer. Financial buyers will use holding companies to make the purchase. These holding companies effectively separate the potential trailing liabilities from swimming upstream to the parent private equity firm or, by extension, to its limited partners.

WHY YOU NEED AN ACCOUNTANT

When you head into a sales transaction, there is a period of time between when the offer is made and the close of the deal. This is known as diligence, which I've mentioned already. But to give a more vivid description, I tell people that diligence is like a proctology exam that never ends. It's not pleasant, and it can last for months. The level of data requests and types of questions you'll receive are intrusive.

Entrepreneurs in a sale process that lasts months need support and people they can hand tasks off to, including some internal resources that are brought into the tent of confidentiality. The more, the merrier when it comes to diligence. In Part Two, we discussed the need to normalize accounting practices, various accounting methods, purpose of the Q of E, and so forth. These are all very good reasons to have a topflight accountant on retainer to help you navigate both the preparation and the actual sale process that we will dig into in Part Four.

During this diligence period, one of the buyer's key focuses is to understand the true financial position of the company being purchased. If you've been running on QuickBooks or don't have a sophisticated finance team, you may be distributing financial statements that have never been audited or reviewed by outside advisors. The accuracy of those statements and the profit calculation methodologies may be suspect. As we discussed earlier in the book, a buyer will need to create these statements if they don't exist and verify them if they do. The former takes longer, and having a position to defend in advance is better than simply responding to the buyer's work later.

The buyer will review your methodologies for reporting and spend a lot of time and money to understand the quality of earnings. Often, a small entrepreneur-led business, even if it is fairly sizable in terms of revenue, will include a variety of personal expenses. We spoke earlier about adjusted EBITDA and pro forma EBITDA, and a competent accountant or transactional advisory services group can help you with this.

SELECTING YOUR FIRMS

You can find tax and accounting help from professionals and firms that come in all shapes and sizes. You'll find small boutique firms where both sides are handled by one professional and their support staff, as well as regional and national firms where personal and company matters are handled by different partners and teams within the firm.

So where do you start? Well, the size of the company being sold is often a good determining factor when it comes to the size of the firm. Let's consult our Sell-Smart-Chart and consider this table below:

REVENUE LOW	REVENUE HIGH	FIRM TYPE LOW SIDE	FIRM TYPE HIGH SIDE
$1 Million	$9 Million	Local Small Firm	Small Regional Firm
$10 Million	$50 Million	Small Regional Firm	Multiregional Firm
$50 Million	$250 Million	Multiregional Firm	Tier 2 National Firm
$250 Million	$2 Billion	Tier 2 National Firm	Big 4 Firm

Note: You may choose one firm, but don't be surprised if you wind up with two partners. Getting personal tax advice, doing a sell-side Q of E, and getting help assembling your business financial story are separate areas of practice.

More sizable firms will typically have specialty practices focused solely on the different needs of business transactions. These transaction advisory service groups provide both the seller and buyer with specialized assistance for items like Q of E reports.

LOCATING TOP FIRMS

When it comes to locating a firm, the top resource I recommend is AccountingToday.com. Accounting Today publishes an annual report that is a golden resource for you. Simply do an internet search for "Accounting Today top 100." You'll quickly locate a downloadable forty-page guide that lists the top accounting firms in the country and includes breakdowns by region. Although larger doesn't always mean better, it's a wonderful free resource that you can use to figure out who is who in your part of the country.

QUESTIONS TO ASK POTENTIAL TAX ADVISORS

- What is your background?
- What is your specialty area of practice?
- What's the typical net worth of the clients you work with?
- How many of your clients are business owners and high-net-worth individuals?
- Have you worked with entrepreneurs who are selling a business?
- Are you able to file taxes in multiple jurisdictions if necessary?
- Do you routinely represent clients who have to file taxes in multiple jurisdictions (if needed)?
- Do you provide audit assistance if I'm ever audited?
- Does your firm have a personal practice to represent me? Do you have a business practice to represent my company? Do you do both, or are you a specialist in one or the other?
- If you're a specialist, does your firm have multiple practices that can take care of the totality of my needs, both as an individual and as a company?
- Can you give me references of high-net-worth individuals like me whom you have represented in the past?

QUESTIONS TO ASK POTENTIAL ACCOUNTANTS

- What is your background?
- What is your specialty area of practice?

- What's the typical revenue of the companies you work with?
- How many of your clients are founder-owned?
- Have you worked with entrepreneurs who are selling a business?
- Do you have experience doing sell-side quality of earnings?
- Can you help me think about preparing my business for sale?
- Can you help me raise my level of sophistication? (This is especially important if you're running QuickBooks without an internal accounting staff and you need to add a layer of professionalism to prepare for the sale.)
- Can you help me think through the types of diligence questions I will receive?
- Can you give me references of high-net-worth individuals and founder-owned companies like me?

KEY TAKEAWAYS

- You need both a competent tax advisor and an accountant. They may (rare) or may not (more common) be the same person. They may (more common) or may not (rare) be from the same firm. But they should not necessarily be picked because they are your friends or golfing buddies who gave you advice in the past. Solid professional advice is critical to achieve the best outcome in a sale transaction.

- Start three years ahead of sale if possible. Begin to normalize your finances and adopt a generally acceptable accounting practice (GAAP), and make sure you have an audit trail. Prepping to sell means a faster transaction and maximum value.

- Leverage online resources like Accounting Today's Top 100 to locate the firms in your area. Leverage your legal advisor to help ferret out the right firm and negotiate the engagement letter.

CHAPTER EIGHT

LAWYERS

There aren't many entrepreneurs on earth who don't have a relationship with an attorney. If you have been in business for decades, there's no chance that you've made it this far without a legal challenge.

Everyone has lawyers they're comfortable doing business with. But selling a business represents a specialty area of legal practice, and competence matters.

Let me use doctors as an analogy. You have most likely been seeing a family physician for a number of years. If you've ever faced a health challenge, the person who operates on you or puts together a plan is typically *not* your family physician. If you need brain surgery, you want the best brain surgeon your policy or money can afford. If you have heart issues, you don't want your dermatologist putting stents inside your chest. There is a time and a place for a general practitioner, and there is a time and a place for a specialist. Everyone gets that concept when it comes to medicine. Unfortunately, it's not as common when it comes to business owners' selection of counsel to represent them in a sale transaction.

WHY YOU NEED A LAWYER

Selling a business is absolutely a specialty area of practice. Rather than hiring a generalist, you want someone who spends their entire career doing nothing but representing buyers and sellers of companies.

Yes, a generalist may be cheaper by the hour than a specialist. But the generalist will take longer to get an agreement negotiated. In addition, they may focus on the wrong elements during the transaction, and their degree of competency will be reflected in the final negotiated agreements. You may have much higher post-closing risks and trailing liabilities if you use a generalist versus a specialist.

Business lawyers who do these transactions also have resources available that they can bring as needed. Every company being sold falls into industry and size categories, and they will have access to up-to-the-minute details on what is commonplace within a transaction contract when you're selling a company in those areas. Contracts change over time, and you need someone who understands the specific elements that are required.

For example, if you're selling a construction company with $50 million in revenue, an attorney can quickly access information to see what is commonly put in a purchase agreement for a $50 million construction company. What are the indemnification clauses like? Those specific clauses may be different by industry and type of product or service manufactured or provided.

There are also sections that govern working capital true-ups after the close—how cash for accounts receivable/payable is normalized and trued up ninety days after a deal closes. Bad legal advice here can cost a seller millions down the road. There is more to agreements than just purchase price—the devil is always in the details.

When I'm in the process of buying a company, I always expect the seller to have competent counsel in place. I don't play games, and I try to always bring a reasonable and customary contract to the table. Not every buyer is like me! If a buyer senses that the counsel on the opposite side of the table isn't competent in this specialty area of practice, they might seek to take advantage. They may try to put in place terms and conditions that are not considered market practice. Often, just a few words can change the balance between buyer-friendly and seller-friendly terms and conditions.

Your counsel has to know what is and is not market. They need to know how to ensure that the agreement is balanced and you don't take on an undue amount of potential liability.

ASSET VERSUS STOCK DEALS

As we mentioned in Chapter Seven, there are two types of deal structures when a company is sold: a stock deal or an asset deal. Your tax advisor is only concerned with the amount of money you will get from the sale and what taxes need to be paid. A lawyer has an opinion on what's better for you as an entrepreneur. This opinion may be based on the type of business, the length of time it has been in business, the cleanliness of the background and history, and so on.

The lawyer's opinion may also be based on potential trailing liabilities after close. You'll need to weigh the advice of both your tax advisor and your attorney to understand the specific differences in your unique situation and then formulate an opinion on the best course to take with the universe of buyers.

SELECTING A FIRM

So where do you start? Well, like with choosing an accountant, the size of the company is often a good determining factor when it comes to the size of the law firm. Let's ask our Sell-Smart-Chart and consider the results in the table below:

REVENUE LOW	REVENUE HIGH	FIRM TYPE LOW SIDE	FIRM TYPE HIGH SIDE
$1 Million	$9 Million	Local Small Firm	Small Regional Firm
$10 Million	$50 Million	Small Regional Firm	Multiregional Firm
$50 Million	$250 Million	Multiregional Firm	Tier 2 National Firm
$250 Million	$2 Billion	Tier 2 National Firm	Top-Tier Firm

Like with accountants, you need to match the tool (and cost) to the job, but you always want a competent advisor! You've spent time, blood, sweat, and tears building your business. Selling is a big transaction. It will be very important to your retirement and livelihood. This is not the time to be cost conscious. Break the mold and recognize that saving money is not a good idea when selling your business or having brain surgery!

Rates for lawyers vary per hour, and all areas of the United States are different. A small generalist firm on the West Coast might charge $400–$600 an hour for a partner's work. A topflight business lawyer at a large firm may charge $1,200–$1,500 per hour.

Yes, those rates are drastically different. However, if you're selling your business of thirty years and the goal is to set you up for retirement, this transaction is critical. You may want to use the cheaper attorney; however, if the expensive specialty partner-negotiated agreement ultimately offers you less risk and more confidence that you have market terms and conditions in the contract, it makes much more sense to go with a specialist.

Law firms and attorneys who specialize in selling businesses do it all day every day, and their practices are very well versed. They understand the standard terms and conditions for a given size and type of transaction and can ensure that the seller gets market terms and the best potential protections in a contract. This is not the place to skimp. Rather, it's the time to use a specialist.

SELECTING TOP FIRMS

When choosing a law firm, the top resource I recommend is the Internet Legal Research Group. ILRG publishes an annual report that is perfect to use when searching for a lawyer. Simply search for "top 350 law firms public legal" on the internet and you'll find their latest rankings of the top 350 law firms in the United States, arranged by number of attorneys. Although the number of attorneys is not necessarily a guarantee of competence, it should give some comfort that all those attorneys have clients. Given number one has 4,720 attorneys and number 350 has 114 attorneys, you can safely say that you'll find both regional and national firms on this list in a city near you.

Another online resource that may be interesting is Vault.com. Do an internet search for "Vault law 100" and the current year. Over 20,000 peers vote for the most respected firms for that year. It's kind of a lawyers' ranking of top firms. (*Note: They are not necessarily arranged by size.*)

For my overseas friends, you'll need to search by your country, but I'm sure similar lists exist in your area too. Most of the top firms on these lists are global and have a presence in many countries.

QUESTIONS TO ASK POTENTIAL LAWYERS

- What is your background?
- What is your specialty area of practice?
- What's the typical net worth of the clients you work with?
- How many of your clients are business owners and high-net-worth individuals?
- Have you worked with entrepreneurs who are selling a business?
- What is the typical size company and transaction that you represent?
- What's the mix between asset and stock deals that you do?
- Are there any specific industries or verticals that you specialize in or that are a unique part of your practice?
- What is your hourly billing rate for a partner?
- What is your hourly billing rate for associates?
- In transactions, how are your hours generally blended between partner and associate?
- What is the general ballpark cost that I could expect to get a transaction done?
- Can you give me references of high-net-worth individuals and founder-owned companies like me?

KEY TAKEAWAYS

- Selling companies is a specialty area of practice. Don't go with your friend or a generalist unless they have extensive experience in business transactions.

- Specialists may charge higher fees per hour, but they will help you complete the transactions in a shorter time with a better outcome that ensures you get the best terms possible.

- Start three years ahead of sale if possible. You can talk to some of your current advisors, lawyers, or tax advisors about the specialty needs that you'll have and ask them for referrals.

- As a seller, you should seek reasonable and customary terms. You are looking for balance and market terms. Any attempt by either party to take advantage often increases hours and runs up the cost.

CHAPTER NINE

INVESTMENT BANKER/ TRANSACTION ADVISOR

So far in Part Three, we've talked about having a competent accountant who can help you prepare your business for sale, finding someone who can offer solid tax advice, and obtaining specialty legal advice.

There's one last player you need to find to build out your team: an investment banker (also referred to as a transaction advisor for smaller companies).

WHY YOU NEED AN INVESTMENT BANKER

Let's take a quick look at the real estate industry. The vast majority of real estate in the United States is sold by realtors or real estate agents. Nearly every transaction has an agent representing the buyer and another agent representing the seller. It's rare to encounter a pure for sale by owner or buy by owner because agents serve a variety of functions. If you're selling a home, your agent helps you put together marketing material and advertise on the multiple listing service (MLS). They hold open house showings for potential buyers who see it as a fit for their size, location, and price requirements. Agents actively work to find the right buyer for your home.

And when they do find that buyer, the agents then handle the paperwork—and the emotions. Real estate agents exist to keep the buyers and sellers apart. Sellers are passionate about their homes. They live there. They may have raised children there and painted murals on their walls. They may have redone the kitchen. They may have added landscaping or a pool. The buyer doesn't typically care about the special carpet or wall color you selected and why. They don't value a house or the memories you have built there. They simply want the best deal. The seller may have a passion for a certain color or wallpaper. The buyer may think your decorating tastes are hideous. There are many reasons to keep buyers and sellers apart in real estate transactions.

The agents facilitate the flow of paperwork, handle opening escrow, and schedule all the inspections. Both sides work to negotiate terms and navigate to the close of escrow. Real estate agents don't get paid unless a transaction is completed.

When you sell your business, your investment banker/transaction advisor essentially does the same thing, only instead of houses, they represent buyers and sellers of businesses.

Investment bankers (or bankers, as we will refer to them from now on) help you prepare your company for sale. They help create marketing materials. They develop a teaser—a one-pager they send to the universe of buyers interested in your particular size and type of company. They assist you in developing the story you bring to the universe of buyers in a confidential information memorandum (CIM) or marketing book. They set up meetings with potential buyers. They help facilitate bids and negotiations. In essence, they help manage the entire process for you. In addition, much like a real estate agent has relationships with mortgage brokers, a banker has relationships with banks and lenders in case the buyer needs financing to close on your sale.

DEVELOPING A UNIVERSE OF BUYERS

A universe of buyers is always better than one buyer. It's the role of the banker to help create that competitive tension by finding a multitude of buyers interested in your business.

This is what they do all day every day.

Bankers work in a variety of business verticals and sizes. One firm may assist in the sales of manufacturing businesses.

Another may focus on healthcare. Another may specialize in retail. Some are broader generalists, but they all focus on the universe of potential buyers. And most larger firms have multiple practices and specialties with separate partners or managing directors heading them up.

The point of all this is that a banker's job requires them to be knowledgeable experts in the industries and verticals they serve. In order to know the universe of potential buyers, they will spend years representing both buyers and sellers in narrowly defined categories. When you hire a banker, you are getting a wealth of specific expertise that the most senior of people have spent a career developing.

This benefits you because the banker will be more efficient with time.

NOTE: INSIDER TIP

Private equity will never sell a company without using an investment banker. Even if they know the buyer, they will still use a banker. Why? There is a higher likelihood of success and a much more controlled experience. So if private equity firms—the most sophisticated buyers on the planet—always use bankers, shouldn't you?

SELECTING A FIRM

No matter your size or industry vertical, there is a banker for you. But how do you know which is the best for you?

I've mentioned several times that you will work with a different size firm depending on the size of the company you are selling. The same holds true with bankers. The smallest of companies, with $1 to $3 million of EBITDA, will typically employ a small local boutique firm. A company with $4 to $10 million of EBITDA will most likely employ a small local firm or a regional firm. A midsize company with $11 to $50 million of EBITDA will probably employ a solid regional or tier-two national firm. A larger company with $51 to $100 million of EBITDA attracts tier-two national firms and starts to get serious attention from top-tier firms. And finally, once a business has an EBITDA of $100 million or more, the largest top investment banks, like Goldman Sachs, Morgan Stanley, JP Morgan, Credit Suisse, and so forth, will be in play.

Most readers of this book will likely be in the lower middle market ($5 to $100 million of revenue) or middle market ($100 to $500 million in revenue). By the time companies are in the upper middle market ($500 million to $1 billion in revenue), they either have already been sold before or have very sophisticated support structures in place.

Fees are typically based on the size of the company being sold. Bankers tend to follow the same rule as real estate agents: they only get paid at the end of a successfully closed transaction. A difference is that investment banks will require an up-front and ongoing payment to cover marketing and expenses, but they get the bulk of their commission when the transaction closes. A real estate agent has you sign a listing agreement when you sell a house. A banker will have you sign an engagement letter.

Transaction fees can vary widely from firm to firm and are based on the total enterprise sale price of a company. Fees as a percentage of the transaction are higher on smaller enterprise values and decline as deals get bigger. Let's put some goalposts around typical ranges by once again consulting our Sell-Smart-Chart:

ENTERPRISE LOW	ENTERPRISE HIGH	FEE RANGE LOW	FEE RANGE HIGH
Under $1 Million	$10 Million	3.0%	6.0%
$10 Million	$25 Million	2.5%	4.0%
$25 Million	$50 Million	2.0%	3.5%
$50 Million	$100 Million	1.5%	3.0%
$100 Million	$250 Million	1.0%	2.0%
$250 Million	$500 Million	0.75%	1.5%
$500 Million	$500 Million And Up	0.50%	1.0%

A company that sells for $1 million might expect to pay a fee of 6 percent or $60,000. A company that sells for $10 million might expect to pay a fee of 3 percent or $300,000. A firm that sells for $500 million might expect to pay $5 million. As companies get bigger, the team working on the project gets bigger, and the activity becomes more intense. But the larger size also means a lower percentage yields a larger payday for the investment banking firm. I tried to use reasonable goalposts for illustrative purposes, but I'm sure I have raised the hackles of many bankers just by trying. The fact is that fees vary widely and go down as deals get bigger.

In addition to base fees, I have also seen success fees added on top. Generally, a base fee is charged up to a certain enterprise amount, and then a sweetener is used at a much higher amount for every dollar over that base ceiling. Example: 1 percent on the first $500 million and then 10 percent for every dollar above. If you were to sell for $525 million, the banker would earn $5 million on the first $500 million, plus an additional $2.5 million on the last $25 million. Success fees are great enticements for truly setting the market.

SELECTING TOP FIRMS

When it comes to locating a firm, turn to your attorney and accountant for some advice. One of the reasons that this is Chapter Nine instead of Chapter Seven or Chapter Eight is you now have a partial team assembled. Your other advisors may be familiar with bankers who sell companies in your area. Ask them for potential referrals to investment banks that fit your size and industry.

Another route is to do an online search of "top investment banks." There are thousands of them, so it's impossible for me to cover all situations and circumstances in this book. Here are a few websites to check out for more information:

Vault.com was mentioned previously for law firms, but it also ranks investment banking firms. Simply search for "Vault most prestigious banking firms" for their latest list.

Mergersandinquisitions.com is another good resource to find listings of top investment banks by tier and category. Simply search for "top investment banks by tier and category" to find their latest report.

QUESTIONS TO ASK POTENTIAL INVESTMENT BANKERS

- What is your background?
- What's the typical industry you work with?
- What's the typical size of company you work with?
- What is the typical EBITDA of the companies you represent?
- What fees do you charge, and how are they structured?
- Talk to me about the sales process you normally run. What are your key steps?
- Do you have any examples of marketing material for recent transactions that you've successfully completed?
- What's your percent success rate?
- Can you give me references?

KEY TAKEAWAYS

- Hire an investment banker/advisor to get the very best outcome for your sale.

- Use the right-sized firm for your specific transaction size and industry or business vertical to obtain the maximum value at close.

- Talk to your legal advisor and accounting advisor to seek potential referrals or introductions.

- Interview several to get a feel for your range of options.

PART THREE WRAP-UP

Selling a business takes the vast majority of entrepreneurs and founders into uncharted territory. Now that your foundational knowledge is building, it's time to delve into obtaining maximum value. We know we need personal tax advice, accounting help, specialty legal advice, and investment banking help. Hopefully, you understand why this additional help is necessary and see the value in assembling a topflight team.

Over my twenty-year career, I have worked with topflight private equity firms that tap topflight talent. I have seen the value that truly competent experts bring to the table for transactions of all sizes. Even though you may be a novice at selling your company, by surrounding yourself with these key players, you'll level any playing field and ensure that the outcome is fair and balanced and that it contains market terms that are reasonable and customary. You'll not only get the top price for your sale, but you'll also minimize the tax ramifications and any trailing liability issues that may arise.

Everyone wins when you wield a highly competent team. Buyers appreciate working with competent professionals. Deals are more predictable, and outcomes are generally better and timelier for all. When I'm a buyer and our team runs into sound advisors on the other side of the deal, I sleep better at night because I can make better predictions about how much capital I'll need to feed the growth engine and when I'll need it to close the deal.

THE SALES PROCESS

In Part One, we looked at the universe of buyers and the types of exit strategies an entrepreneur can employ. In Part Two, we talked about preparing the business for sale. In Part Three, we started building our team of advisors. Now in Part Four, our focus shifts to the sales process.

You know how you built your business. But do you know the steps involved in virtually every banker-assisted sale process? Do you know your role and how to instill confidence in the buyers so that they bid high because they want to own your business?

You will soon!

A typical sale process generally takes four to six months from the time you engage a banker to the time you sit at a closing table. The biggest variable has to do with the length of time a buyer needs to get through diligence. You can assist by being a prepared seller.

In my world, I have seen the sale of a company with a purchase price of $500 million completed in as little as three weeks. I have also seen a small deal with a purchase price of only $10 million take over a year to complete. If you've made it this far, you will be well prepared, and we will assume four to six months as a typical timeline.

WHEN SHOULD YOU LAUNCH A PROCESS?

Although there's no hard-and-fast rule about when you should start the sales process, I will tell you this: you shouldn't target a deal to close during the holidays. Working forward from when you start, you want to complete a transaction before the holidays or plan to launch after the holidays. Ideally, you start the sales process early in the year and seek to be done by summer or third quarter at the latest. The new year is the perfect time to start because everyone is back at work and no longer focused on closing their year.

Deals done during the holidays suffer hits to momentum because people become distracted. If buyers have had a good year, they are less likely to stretch late in Q4, and if bankers have made their money, they're not quite as hungry facilitating the sale. Lenders tend to be less aggressive when pricing deals because they've most likely already achieved their lending quotas. Simply stated, there's too much downside risk and not enough upside gains in a Q4-launched deal.

By early Q1, everyone is starting the year over; buyers, bankers, and lenders come out of the holidays with a renewed hunger to hit the new year's aggressive growth numbers. Since we are talking about timing, I should also mention that half of Wall Street goes on summer vacation in August, and activity drops off in August. So although it's okay to have August in your deal window, I wouldn't launch a project or target a close in August because your target deal and financing audience might not be around to participate with their A-team.

CHAPTER TEN

MARKETING AND PROCESS FLOW

In Chapter Nine, we touched on the analogy that selling a company is like selling a home and that a banker's role is like that of a real estate agent. We're going to expand that to picture a funnel. When selling a home, your agent starts by sitting down with you to assess your goals, evaluate comps, and come up with a target listing price. They then create marketing material and put your house on the MLS, which is the top of the funnel, to allow the mass universe of potential buyers browsing the MLS listings on Zillow, Realtor.com, and so on to discover you.

As the marketing and open house events start to draw people in, the funnel of potential buyers gets smaller. Together, you and your agent zero in on a set of buyers and continue to narrow your focus as you work through the offer process, inspections, and financing. Sometimes, when you sell a home, multiple families get into a bidding war and hopefully drive up the price to the maximum value. Either way, at the end, you have a successful sale where hopefully both buyer and seller walk away happy.

This process is similar to selling a company.

START WITH TRANSPARENCY

The banker generally starts by spending time with you and your management team. This requires that your team knows what's happening.

Most entrepreneur-led companies make a sale process confidential. This is understandable but can potentially limit buyer access to the company during a sale process. I think the benefits of transparency far outweigh the risks. Employees were not born yesterday. If they see you aging, I guarantee the future disposition of their fearless leader has crossed their mind a time or two. Transparency lets me involve more people in the sale process and aids in getting diligence done faster. It also helps me use my home-court advantage (which we will discuss in an upcoming sidebar on the value of a "sexy headquarters").

So how can you be transparent? I keep *all* of my employees in the loop. I discuss what it means to be privately held—either individually or by institutional shareholders. I tell them that at some point over the next few years, I'll be bringing in a new set of shareholders. That buyer will come in, and we will keep growing. Five years later, a new sales transaction will take place. This relay race will continue until, someday down the road, we are too big to remain private and we potentially hit the public markets.

Note: When I say I keep all of my employees in the loop, I truly mean all of my employees! All 3,000 employees at CoolSys know we are privately held, what that means, and how our company will go through a transition of shareholders at varying points along our journey. If they are paying attention to my communications, they get regular updates along the way and know exactly when it's time to say goodbye to one group of shareholders and welcome another.

BUILD YOUR TEAM

Now that you've become more transparent, you need to bring on some trusted members of the team to help you dive into the sale and work with your banker. You'll want at least one person from finance, one from operations, and one from sales and marketing, depending on the size of the company.

This small team will help you while interfacing with the universe of buyers. The more people who can articulate your vision and assist with all the diligence requests, the faster the process will move and the better the buyer will feel.

Imagine you are selling a car, but the potential buyers are not allowed to see or drive the car. It's hard to get top dollar based on a verbal description of a vehicle. I think this holds true with companies. Your efforts can't only be financial spreadsheets and secret meetings with buyers in hotel conference rooms. Transparency helps you get maximum value.

Your banker will spend time with you and your leadership team to make sure everyone is ready for the sale. They will help you all prepare for buyer presentations, work with you on how to deliver the content, and serve as your personal coach. I have been doing this for twenty years, and I still do dry runs with bankers, prepping for questions and discussing how to present specific information. Selling a business is a team sport, and the more you practice, the better your game day results.

The banker will then dig into the business, look at the financial statements, and determine the potential universe of buyers based on your input and the future you desire.

These elements all play into the crafting of your story.

ONE-PAGE TEASER

One of the first pieces of marketing material that your banker will create is a one-page teaser. It's as simple as it sounds: a teaser that includes a high-level overview of the company, history, and industry. Your banker won't include the company name yet; rather, they will assign a project name. A plumbing company might be called Project Drāno—a clue into the industry but with no specific details. The last time I sold CoolSys, the bankers used Project Iceman. It had a nice ring to it and an air of mystery. For a large refrigeration company, the reference to ice and cold was certainly fitting.

The one-page teaser is colorful and catchy. It uses a combination of words, charts, and graphs, along with contact information for the banker's deal team. For example:

> We're excited to announce we are representing Project Drāno, a large residential and commercial plumbing company that has 300 trucks on the road and conducts business in five different states. They service these customer verticals: ____. Revenue has grown from X to Y over the last three years. EBITDA has gone from X to Y. The founder is engaged and plans to roll over. Please let us know within the next two weeks if you have a potential interest in this company.

This teaser is then sent out to the universe of potential buyers who might be interested in purchasing the company. Locating these buyers is why you hired a banker—their job is to research and understand specific industries and verticals. Strategic buyers are probably in the same or a similar industry and looking to expand their market share and build scale. Financial buyers will be looking to use your company as a platform or as part of a buy and build. Your banker may focus on companies in your industry, private equity groups that are active in this type of vertical, or other similar commercial or residential service-based businesses that might be interested. Ultimately, the teaser will be distributed to all potential buyers for the business—anywhere from thirty to one hundred buyers.

Teasers allow the banker to start to fill the funnel. I get teasers all the time. Good bankers know the types of companies I buy and reach out to me with pertinent opportunities that fit my requirements. Bankers firing broad scatter shots also send me teasers, often for industries or verticals that don't fit, but occasionally they are spot on. Although these teasers are not all posted in one place—like a real estate agent's MLS listing—the passing of teasers between advisors and the universe of buyers is like a virtual MLS.

Note to VC investors and entrepreneurs: Why isn't there an MLS of sorts for teasers that qualified buyers can use to scan the universe of companies currently for sale or running a process? That sure would simplify all the teaser blasting that goes on every day.

NONDISCLOSURE AGREEMENT

While the teaser is being distributed, you will begin drafting a fairly simple nondisclosure agreement (NDA). This may include the work of multiple resources to finalize. Expect the banker and your legal advisor (either inside or outside counsel) to participate.

This NDA is a confidentiality agreement with fairly benign terms designed to protect your company's information. Generally, there is little risk or concern of a financial buyer learning too much in the sale process. However, if there is a strategic buyer in your area and demographic, the NDA may be more targeted and specific. Sellers often have some concerns when it comes to the sharing of customer and key employee data. Don't worry. There are multiple ways around this problem.

The banker will very quickly whittle down the buyer list to the ones who are potentially in play. Perhaps they send out fifty to one hundred teasers and narrow the universe of buyers down to twenty-five who respond and are interested in learning more about your company.

At this point, the banker will send out the NDA.

CIM/CIP

After the NDAs are signed, it's time to release your confidential information memorandum (CIM) or confidential information presentation (CIP). What's the difference? It either comes in the form of a Microsoft Word-originated PDF document (CIM) or a PowerPoint-generated PDF presentation (CIP).

The CIM/CIP is a fifty- to one-hundred-page document that delves into the opportunity in extensive detail. It includes very detailed information about your company, what you do, your products and services offered, how big the addressable market is, how the company is managed, the number of employees, and employees' average tenure. An org chart shows the leadership team and their years of experience in the industry. It also includes information about the market served, growth over time, prospects for the future, and growth projections. The buyer universe wants to know the plans for the next five years and how the company—with a new owner—can exploit additional opportunities in the marketplace.

Your banker will create this document for you. You should have asked for sample teasers and CIPs/CIMs when evaluating bankers. You'll see a tremendous amount of similarity between those examples and yours. There is a tried-and-true template at play.

At this point, there has been no indication of valuation from buyers. The teaser gets them interested. The CIM/CIP gives them very detailed information ahead of the fireside chat below.

FIRESIDE CHAT

Of the fifty teasers sent out, twenty-five potential buyers came back and signed NDAs. CIMs/CIPs were sent out, and you talked to the banker and decided that eighteen of those buyers were likely to be competitive bidders, with perhaps ten considered most likely to be aggressive. The next step in the sales process is to participate in a series of one-on-one conversations, sometimes called fireside chats, with those top ten buyers. The fireside chats could take place in person (pre-COVID-19) or via phone or video calls (most likely in today's world). The goal is to answer any questions for the potential buyer and to honestly make them feel special.

Note: The term "fireside chat" is a reference to evening radio addresses to the nation by US President Franklin D. Roosevelt back in the 1930s and '40s. In those pre-television days, Americans sat around the fireplace and listened to his broadcast via radio in a personal and private setting. Roosevelt used this method to develop a one-on-one relationship with millions of Americans simultaneously. You'll follow in his footsteps and make a subset of the remaining buyers feel special about being the potential partner to your business.

During a fireside chat, conversations will stay high level.

This is the time for your canned elevator pitch on the business. At this stage, the buyer is developing an internal model for your business. They are building projections and trying to determine how this company might grow during their hold period (for financial buyers) or what the long-term synergies might look like (for strategic buyers). You won't go down too many rabbit holes, but fireside chats might yield some intel around the type of questions you are likely to field during upcoming management meetings.

IOI

After the fireside chats, your banker will ask the potential buyers for an indication of interest (IOI). This is typically a nonbinding bid expressed in a range of numbers because the buyers still don't have quite enough information to give a single number. When a process is competitive, buyers use a range primarily to ensure they make it to the next round and don't get dismissed. Bankers are always talking to buyers, so chances are that by the time IOIs start to fly, they've already had some valuation discussions, and the banker has tipped a hand as to what it takes to remain in the game.

The IOI may also include indications of how the buyer plans to finance the company, how quickly they can close on the sale, the disposition of the founder, and so on. Buyers at the IOI stage sell you on their financial strength and ability to close to build credibility and show that they are qualified and a good potential partner. IOIs are generally light on detail because buyers are mindful not to alienate a seller. Typical IOIs will be one to four pages in length and tell you how impressed the buyers are with your business and how they would like to be the partner to drive you to the next level.

At this point, your banker will discuss the bids with you, and together you will thin the herd to move forward with a select group of people.

Note: In my experience as a seller, when IOIs come in, I'm looking at the absolute range of all bids (lowest to highest) and the spread of each individual bid. I like to lay them out as stacked horizontal line graphs to see how wide they are, how they intersect one another, and where the midpoints line up. I like to see narrow bid ranges from each buyer. That tells me they get the story. If all the bids have a wide spread in their individual ranges, that is an indication your buyers don't quite know how to value the business.

At this stage, you should start to see some separation from the herd. There will inevitably be some buyers who value your business differently from the rest. You want to keep an eye on those but bring forward enough bidders to keep the process competitive. You may lose a few during the management meetings, so err on the side of caution by having enough around to keep the competitive tension high.

A seller's spirits are pretty high at this point, but try to set aside excitement or depression. There are still opportunities for the banker to work the price up. I have seen deals close higher than the first round of IOIs, and I've also seen lower. Sellers should be emotionless if possible because it can break either way following the management meetings when refreshed bids are received.

MANAGEMENT MEETINGS

Teasers went out to fifty potential buyers. NDAs were signed, and the CIM/CIP went out to twenty-five. The field narrowed to eighteen by seller choice, after which we held fireside chats with ten. The first-round IOIs have been received, and the buyer universe has narrowed again to the top eight to ten prospects deemed most likely to get to the finish line.

During this time, potential buyers have been building their investment models and considering the price they will pay and the value proposition that this asset brings to the table.

Strategic buyers focus on a model that works through bending the revenue growth curve, cross-selling new customers, harnessing cost synergies, receiving value from any new strategic capabilities, building density in an existing market, and developing an opinion on how this business—when combined with the mothership—will yield a classic "one plus one yields something higher than two" outcome.

A financial buyer considers the potential growth trajectory. They determine how much money they will invest to buy the company and improve it and then what return they can make when they sell it five years later. Generally, they're trying to solve for a three-times multiple of invested capital (MOIC). To learn more about MOIC, and internal rate of return (IRR), please refer to *The Private Equity Playbook* where we talked about these in greater detail.

After they've expressed their IOI, buyers come in for management meetings and spend half a day with the management team. So far, the buyer has only been exposed to the founder or CEO during the fireside chats. At this point, they want to see if this company has sound processes in place and if the leadership team knows what they are doing and are engaged and ready to execute. When I'm a seller, I typically bring five or six team members with me. Bigger companies include top leaders in finance, operations, HR, sales, and potentially IT. Smaller companies tend to bring fewer people with them, but ideally it would not just be the owner. I have seen some founder-owned companies break the management meeting into two sections: a broader group followed by an executive session with only the main shareholders who are active in the business for some private conversations around any sensitive matters.

Management meetings often include dinner the night before with one buyer, followed by a morning of meetings. This is followed by an afternoon and dinner with a new buyer. This process continues until all remaining buyers get a meeting.

Meetings tend to be approximately four hours in length. A portion of time (thirty minutes is typical) is set aside for the buyer to give an overview of who they are, why they are interested, and how your universe will be better if you choose them. This is a great time for you to ask some questions about the buyer and their plans and vision for the company and its leadership after the close. You should think of questions ahead of time, and don't be afraid to send a list in advance of the meeting. This is a big deal for you—you might have a list of ten pertinent questions you'd like answered. Here are some examples.

EXAMPLE QUESTIONS FOR FINANCIAL BUYERS

- What are the total assets under management (AUM) at your firm?
  - AUM is a key indicator of the size of a firm.
- What fund are you currently investing out of?
  - Fund one means new firm, while fund five means they've been around the block for at least a few decades.
- How large is your current fund?
- What is the typical MOIC you underwrite when making a platform investment?

- Past performance is not a guarantee of future return, but it's an indicator of how the firm has performed. The higher the number, the better you can expect your rollover to do.
- Talk to me about management incentive equity—how much do you allocate, and how does it work?
  - It should be at least 10 percent; I have seen 0 percent on the low side and as high as 14 percent on the high side.
  - There are many styles, so understanding how theirs works is important.
- What is your expectation around rollover investment?
  - Most firms expect entrepreneurs to roll over 10 to 50 percent, and 30 percent is typical.
- Do you pay a preferred yield on equity?
  - This sounds good on the surface but has a negative impact on the management incentive pool because that stock is paid after equity and preferred is paid.
- Do you charge quarterly or annual management fees at the company level?
  - Management fees charged at the company level hurt incentive equity returns. This cash going to the private equity firm could be used to pay down debt. I've seen up to $2 million per year charged on larger companies. You'll find the industry transitioning to not charging fees, but it's a mix in today's world, with several firms still following the old practice.
- What is your typical hold period for an investment?

- Expect three to seven years, with an average of five years.
- Can I speak to some entrepreneurs you have worked with in the past?
  - Perhaps ask to speak to some where the investment went well and a few where the CEO had to be replaced.

EXAMPLE QUESTIONS FOR STRATEGIC BUYERS

- What is the long-term vision of your company?
- What is the strategy on acquisitions at your company, and how does mine fit into that narrative?
- Do you intend to turn the lights off after the acquisition?
  - As we stated earlier, there are two types of strategic buyers. You should know well in advance what their intent is for you and the team after close.
- What changes should my employees and I expect after closing if you are the buyer?
  - Benefits
  - Retirement plans
  - Banking
  - Level of autonomy
- What synergies are you planning to harvest after close?
- How will any impacted employees be treated as synergies are realized?
- Is there an opportunity to make a rollover investment?
- What is your culture and level of employee engagement?

- How many strategic acquisitions have you made?
- Can I speak to some former owners who have sold their business to you?

There are far too many potential questions to list them all here. Work with your advisory team to understand the pertinent questions for your specific situation, and make sure you get them all answered as a part of the sale process. In addition to getting maximum value at exit, your goal should also be to partner with a buyer that is the best fit for you and your employees after close. Once sold, you don't get any takebacks—you are stuck!

SEXY HEADQUARTERS

Over the last ten years, I have been a regular guest speaker at multiple local major colleges and universities. My primary topics include entrepreneurial leadership and private equity, and the typical audience includes the business school's fully employed or executive MBA candidates. As part of my standard routine, I conduct a spot poll and ask the entire audience, "How many of you own an Apple product?" Invariably, 90 percent of hands go up in the air. Then I ask, "Of those of you with your hands in the air, how many of you, somewhere in your house, have the box that the Apple product came in?"

Nearly 90 percent of the hands stay up. I then follow up with, "How many of you own a Dell computer and still have a Dell computer box in your closet?" Laughter follows because nobody ever keeps the Dell box.

Apple did a great job of creating an affinity for its packaging. I'm guilty of it too. Somewhere in my closet, I've got a bunch of Apple boxes for every active product I own.

I use that analogy when I design and build a corporate headquarters: I want to build an Apple box.

When the universe of buyers comes to visit during the management meetings, the party generally consists of a partner, a mid-level person, and a few analysts or junior players in the private equity world. Strategic buyers also send a few senior folks along with a cadre of more junior people from their M&A team. These groups descend on your business, and you want them to enter, look around, and get a good feel for the asset for sale.

When your headquarters looks like an Apple box, it changes the dynamic. TVs on the wall rotate through slides of installation examples and customer testimonials. A mural displays the company's mission and vision. Core values are documented all over the wall. There's a museum display of bathtubs dating back for the last 200 years showing the evolution over time. They enter and say, "Wow, this place is cool! I wasn't expecting this. I was expecting an old dumpy plumbing company, but they have a great lobby."

When they look down at their spreadsheets, they're still looking at earnings and multiples that the industry trades at, but now they're wondering what premium they will have to pay to own your asset. Company headquarters can be just like that Apple box when it comes to getting maximum value at exit.

My research has shown that an innovative headquarters and environment adds approximately one turn of value on a large company and up to two turns on a smaller company. If a company sells for a ten-times multiple, my Apple box HQ helps me sell for eleven times or more!

This has nothing to do with the price per square foot that you invest in a headquarters. It has to do with building a compelling environment that talks about who the company is, what the company believes, and what the company does. It speaks of employee engagement, and that adds significant value.

I typically spend $1 million or more outfitting a headquarters environment for any company I run that has $250 to $600 million of revenue. If a company has $50 to $150 million of EBITDA and you can get one extra turn because of a very compelling environment, $1 million should be worth it to build out an amazing headquarters. This Apple box also helps with employee retention and attracting top new talent. It creates a home-court advantage in a sale process and is one of the most important investments an entrepreneur can make.

Let's face it, most entrepreneurs are very cost conscious and tend to have very understated headquarters. They don't tell stories. They are older facilities. This is a huge missed opportunity when it comes to getting maximum value at exit.

REFRESHED BIDS

After the management meetings, the banker will seek refreshed bids from the buyers. This bid will no longer be a range; it will now be a hard number. IOIs become LOIs (letters of intent), and now many salient deal points start to be included or at least known and communicated. These are still nonbinding, but those at the lead end of the pack will start to separate from the rear.

Your banker should be building competitive tension and pushing those valuations to the top end of the range. They will guide the buyers upward in order to maximize the enterprise value. There will be some back-and-forth discussions, and often buyers will be looking for angles to become the sole remaining buyer. By this time, the buyer universe has invested a great deal of time and effort but perhaps not yet a large amount of money (that comes next in diligence. Buyers don't like to invest a lot of money in deals that don't get to a closing table). At this stage, buyers are looking for exclusivity and a defined time period to close. Bankers want to keep competitive tension; buyers want exclusivity. These are fine lines to walk and the reason you hire a banker in the first place.

EXCLUSIVITY

Your buyer universe limits down to one who asks for exclusivity or two who ask for exclusivity but are granted semi-exclusivity. Often, the banker will stage the parties in such a fashion that the top dog gets a chance to truncate the ongoing process if they can perform quickly. The risk of granting exclusivity is that you lose the other bidders and the party that has exclusivity may not close. Once again, this is why you hire a banker.

DILIGENCE

Here is where the team you assembled earns their keep.

The buyer has a fiduciary responsibility to really dig in and make sure they understand all the potential liabilities. Diligence is not only on the company but also you. The buyer will conduct criminal background checks and try to learn everything about your history. If there are any skeletons in your closet, now is the time to bring that knowledge to the forefront. It's not unusual to encounter a seller who has had a DUI or some other offense in their background. In my experience, I'd estimate that for around 20 to 30 percent of companies I have bought, the founder has had something on their record. Don't sweat it—it's not a big deal. There's probably a larger issue if you have a felony conviction for a Ponzi scheme. Sellers reflect broader society at large, so a clean record isn't necessarily a requirement; however, honesty is expected. If you have had any issues, be transparent.

Multiple tracks will take place in diligence concurrently:

- Finance track to make sure your earnings are accurate.
- HR and pay practices track where they dig into wage and hour, employee misclassifications, retirement plans, turnover, and culture and ensure you are following employment law in the different cities and states you conduct business.
- Commercial liability insurance track.
- Sales, customers, and marketing track.
- Technology track that includes ERP, infrastructure, data, security, and so forth.
- Legal track that includes drafting agreements as well as discovery around any potential trailing liabilities, lawsuits your company has had, and so forth.

During a typical sale process, your banker will help you and your assembled team prepare for diligence. The banker will dedicate an online space known as a data room where you and your team will upload company-generated information into folders so the buyers in diligence can access the information they need to conduct a thorough review of the company. Data gathering will start before the teasers go out, and by the time buyers get access, hopefully it will be fairly robust.

Often, with the release of a CIP/CIM, buyers will be let into the data room and exposed to the first level of data to help support their review that leads to their initial IOI. Sometimes a "financial pack" of information will also be released with the CIP/CIM to help buyers dig into the first layer of detail.

Diligence is expensive for buyers. It's fairly common for diligence to cost several hundred thousand on a small deal and several million on a large one. While researching for this book, I looked at several deals I have done as a strategic buyer and those done by my buyers that then became partners when I was a seller. For deals where I was a strategic buyer and paid around $20 million in enterprise value, my typical diligence costs were in the neighborhood of $400,000 (2 percent). For deals where I sold to financial buyers at an average price of $500 million, they paid around $7.5 million in total diligence costs (1.5 percent). So I have enough experience to say that on average, a buyer will spend around 1.5 to 2 percent of the sale price on diligence costs to get to the closing table. I think that helps show why people want exclusivity. It's okay to pay when you win a deal, but it gets really expensive if you come up empty.

PURCHASE AGREEMENT AND CLOSING

Buyers that are trying to close quickly or truncate the process will typically start all diligence tracks concurrently, as we discussed above. This includes the legal track, where a purchase agreement gets drafted. In a normal process, the actual purchase contract negotiation starts as the buyer gets comfortable with the quality of earnings.

Legal fees are a big part of diligence costs. Buyers don't like to draft contracts and get the lawyer taxicab meters running unless they believe the probability of close is high. That probability goes up dramatically as financial numbers are solidified by the Q of E, so Q of E is priority number one when diligence starts and is often a tollgate to the high cost of lawyers that follows.

As we have discussed, purchase agreements are an asset deal or stock deal. Each deal contains a customary set of features, including a description of what is being sold, who is selling, and who is buying and a basic set of parameters around trailing liabilities—who owns them and for how long, as well as what is included and excluded.

Basic agreements typically contain some baskets and mechanisms for truing up things like accounts receivable, payable, payroll, benefits, and so on that are collectively known as working capital adjustments. Remember that companies are an ongoing concern—you can't stop the day-to-day to consummate a deal cleanly. Some elements will need accounting attention after the deal closes to turn pre-close working estimates into historically known facts ninety days after closing.

A seller can expect a portion of the sale proceeds to be held back in escrow for a period of time—typically around 10 to 20 percent for twelve to twenty-four months. This capital becomes the source of funds to true up any post-close cleanup. Any funds remaining after the escrow period ends are released back to the seller.

One of the biggest parts of the contracts (and a source of seller headaches) is the attached schedules that include the details of the purchase agreement. The purchase agreement verbiage is high level. Example: "All vehicles owned by the company and identified in schedule A are included." In my current company, that would be 1,900 vehicles. So schedule A would contain 1,900 line items spelling out the make, model, year, VIN, approximate mileage, and so forth. The agreement stays short, but the schedules provide the detail and are incorporated as attachments to the agreement. In deals I have been involved with, closing schedules are where deals are often delayed. Everything must be spelled out. I always find it helpful for sellers to receive a template for each schedule from the buyer so they know what data is needed and the format it should be provided in.

In addition to the basic purchase agreement, other legal documents may need to be negotiated, such as real property leases, consulting or employment agreements, and noncompetes. Some of these may be referred to in the purchase agreement, but they are still separate agreements that need to be negotiated before closing can take place.

Because you hired a competent lawyer in Part Three of the book, I'll leave this introductory point to stimulate your thinking and suggest you explore your specific situation with your attorney and let them fill in the blanks on the agreements and features you will need to review.

TIMELINE

Every sales process, although having similar major elements, will contain a variety of nuances based on your company's size. My example process here would typically apply to companies with an EBITDA of a few million dollars in size and up. When companies are smaller than that, investment banks get traded out for brokers or business advisors, and their processes are a little more intimate. The smaller a company, the more likely the main process steps will be less robust. There will likely be fewer horses in the race—the process will usually be conducted with one or two buyers at a time. They will still try to create a competitive tension, but a small owner-operated business with a few employees won't have the same number of players.

Below is a table showing a timeline of typical activity in a sale process, starting with the hiring of an investment banker. Timelines can vary wildly. I have seen some processes take less than half this time and some take more than a year.

ACTIVITY	TYPICAL TIME ALLOTTED	TOTAL TIME ELAPSED
Interview and hire banker	4 weeks	4 weeks
Marketing prep, teaser done, and CIM start	2 weeks	6 weeks
Teasers out, NDAs signed	2 weeks	8 weeks
CIMS/CIPS sent out	2 weeks	10 weeks
Fireside chats	1 week	11 weeks
IOIs due	1 week	12 weeks
Management meetings	2 weeks	14 weeks
Q&A calls—refreshed bids due	2 weeks	16 weeks
Diligence process/ contracts/financing	10 weeks	26 weeks
Final prep and closing	1 week	27 weeks

Diligence can by far be the longest part of the process. Often, in order to get exclusivity, the banker will want to see diligence conducted over a limited time frame and require the buyer to quickly reaffirm the bid price. The banker might be holding back other buyers without jettisoning them in order to let a party run ahead if the purchase price warrants their attempt to truncate the process.

The last time I took a company out to market, the universe of buyers sought to immediately preempt a process to prevent it from even beginning. This phenomenon is fairly common in today's world. The banker ran a normal process up to the release of the CIP and then allowed the top bidder to run forward. In order to get that accommodation, the buyer put down a number that was high enough to warrant ending the process and agreed to pay 100 percent cash at closing with no financing contingency. The buyer also agreed to a two-week diligence period to affirm their price and another week to get to a closing table. It was a $500 million deal that closed in three weeks from the time exclusivity was granted.

KEY TAKEAWAYS

- Selling a company requires strong marketing material.

- The sales process has a very structured and methodical flow.

- Having a good investment banker or advisor will make the process smooth.

- You obtain maximum value by trusting your advisory team and letting them work their process alongside you.

- Buyers are very sophisticated; your advisory team helps raise your game to their level and protects you from being outmatched.

CHAPTER ELEVEN

INTERACTING WITH BUYERS

This chapter will focus on you and how you need to act as an individual when engaging with the universe of buyers. In the sales process, we discussed that you will be a part of the fireside chats, management meetings, and dinners associated with those meetings. This will be a short chapter, but due to its importance, I wanted to focus on it as a separate matter rather than bury it inside another.

So let's talk about you.

THE FIRESIDE CHAT

The fireside chat is probably the first opportunity for the buyer to interact with you directly. It's generally just you and your banker talking to two or three people from the buyer side—the partner or mid-level executive and an analyst (for private equity or a financial buyer) or someone from the business development team and someone from finance or operations (for a strategic buyer).

The fireside chat is where your elevator pitch comes out. You need to come across as confident but not arrogant. You need to be engaging and focused. You need to practice that pitch, prepare for likely questions, and be thoughtful, engaging, and passionate about your business and its story.

Your banker will typically sit in on any meeting and kick you under the table (figuratively, electronically, or literally if you are together) or ask for a break if you are off track or struggling. They may even tee up some softballs when you miss a key point. They are there to help you and coach you. The chat focuses on you and the company, so they can't do it for you, but they will be helpful. They will also take notes and make sure to capture areas of questioning to help better prepare for subsequent meetings.

MANAGEMENT MEETING

During the four-hour management meeting, you and your leadership team are on your feet, giving a presentation to the next potential owner. Public speaking skills are imperative. You need to be a leader, not just a manager. Managers are very effective at handling the affairs of an organization. They manage *things*. Leaders inspire *people*.

Leaders who can engage an audience go so much further than someone who is simply a good manager. In order to get maximum value, you need to inspire the buyer universe and tell a compelling story with conviction.

What did Barack Obama sell the American people? He sold them hope. What the heck is hope? You can't put hope in a box or put it on a shelf. Hope is intangible. But he articulated his vision so clearly that he easily won the election. You need to sell buyers a box of hope for the future, and if you can, you're going to get a lot more value for your company.

I mention this because many people are scared of public speaking. They don't like standing in front of a crowd. They freeze. But it's worth its weight in gold to get over those fears and focus on telling a story with passion and conviction.

You don't have to be passionate about every aspect of your business. You just need to be passionate about your people and how you take care of them. You need to be passionate about taking care of your customers and how that leads to repeat business and organic growth.

So if you're bad at public speaking, now is the time to work through those fears and build your presentation skills. Some people are born with an ability to stand up, talk, and entertain. Others have to work really hard at it. If you're one of the latter, these are skills you can build. You can take classes or join a local Toastmasters group. Growing up, I was the class clown whose smart mouth was always getting him in hot water. That became my ultimate superpower—the ability to articulate an engaging shared vision that others would line up to follow. In my case, the army smacked the smartass out of me and then added discipline and leadership to my personal toolkit.

Another way to build these skills is to head to a local church that has an engaging minister or pastor. Early in my career, I visited many different churches to hear the ministers speak. They have a vast amount of talent when it comes to convincing their parishes to believe. Take note of their skills and try to emulate them.

There's a rule of thumb in public speaking: every single slide in your presentation represents one hour of practice. If you have a thirty-page presentation, it is worth your time to lock yourself up for thirty hours. Stand in front of a mirror and practice, practice, practice. Don't just read from the text on the slides. Use them as eye candy to wow the crowd but then expand on the three key points you'd like to make on each slide. If there are six points, the slide needs to be split into two. By hitting the main points consistently, you'll do well, and each one will likely trigger three more subpoints.

Management presentations are like unrecorded stories of old passed on through the generations: although told slightly differently throughout time, the main points of the story remain intact. Keep in mind that if you have a thirty-slide presentation and five people presenting, you may each only need to present and become really good at six slides. If you are a weak speaker, expanding your tent of confidentiality to include more leaders can help you shore up the presentation.

When I am participating in presentations as a seller, I like to play games with my leadership team in order to calm the moment and relieve the stress. We play "management meeting bingo." Together, we create odd phrases or word groupings that earn points when spoken aloud. If you can weave these bonus words or phrases into your presentation, you earn points. Scores are tallied, and there are winners and losers. Instead of being stressed out, people are smiling and being creative on their feet.

If you're presenting to fifteen different groups of buyers, it's critical that you put in the time to practice. You absolutely have to ace it time after time. You want maximum value? You have to talk with passion about the business you built, how much it has grown, the team of people you've assembled, and how you're going to continue to grow using their money over the next five years. You have to sell your buyers hope. Tell them you're committed to this journey and there is nothing more important in life that you can do.

DO NOT LET YOUR GUARD DOWN

There's a reason the potential buyers want to have a meal with you. They want to catch you with your guard down when you're not in the corporate boardroom, presentation room, or hotel meeting room. They want to see you in a social setting with a drink in your hand—if you're so inclined—to see what else they can learn. Who else is in the process, and can they get any competitive indication of values others have offered? They want to see how you act and what else you will divulge. You are on display at all times. Social settings are hard for a banker to control. Side conversations occur in an unmonitored fashion.

YOUR BEHAVIOR CAN KILL THE DEAL

I recently acted as an advisor to a private equity group interested in buying a company in an industry I had experience with. I attended the management meeting via video chat, and the buyers attended in person. I asked my questions, and they asked their questions. The management team did a great job of presenting. I thought highly of the team. Later that night, the private equity team took the management team to dinner. The founder of the company had several martinis during a three-hour dinner. He had trouble talking and walking, and he got up from dinner and drove home.

That killed the deal. The private equity team no longer cared about the business and how good it looked on paper. Here was a man who clearly had a problem and was willing to take the risk of being intoxicated and driving home. They offered to call him an Uber, and he refused. What financial buyer wants to take on that risk?

Seems pretty basic, right? You are always on display in a sale process. Be mindful that anything you do or say can and will be used in the buyer's internal value conversation. You are either racking up intangible points or giving them away. Industry multiples and competition determine price ranges, but these intangible points add potential value stretch and can help impact where you'll fall in that range.

KEY TAKEAWAYS

- Be prepared and on point with messaging.

- Get comfortable speaking in front of others and show passion for your business.

- Public speaking skills are very important to maximum value.

- For each slide you present, spend one hour practicing in an empty room.

- Be on your guard and be mindful of side conversations and social drinking at dinners.

CHAPTER TWELVE

ROLLOVER INVESTING AND RESIDUAL INCOME STREAMS

This chapter will focus on additional opportunities for entrepreneurs or sellers to maximize the financial opportunity ahead of them. Most entrepreneurs think of a sale process as being one and done. They sell the business, cash out their chips, and put the money in the bank. If they aren't the sole owner and controller of the business, they certainly don't want to invest in it anymore.

But again, it depends on your buyer. Some strategic buyers may want you to join the team. A financial buyer absolutely wants and needs you to stay on. They also want you to be a rollover investor because then you've got skin in the game and will work toward collective success.

ROLLOVER INVESTING PERCENTAGES

I recently talked to a partner from one of the largest private equity firms on the planet. During the conversation, he revealed that they expect the seller of an entrepreneur-founded business to roll over at least 50 percent of the proceeds or they are not interested in the purchase.

Some financial buyers will settle for a 10 to 15 percent investment, but typically they want to see 20 to 30 percent. This shows you have conviction and passion to grow the business for them as a new majority shareholder. If you take all your money off the table, you might disconnect or tune out. Then they're left with a company and no leader.

When the percentage of rollover becomes contentious, I like to remind a financial buyer that the average private equity buyout fund will buy eight to ten platform companies, meaning no more than 13 percent of their fund invests in any one asset. Why? Diversification. You are selling to diversify your asset base too. You are getting older; you need to get some chips off the table. You're saying, "Don't worry, Buyer. Between your incentive equity and my rollover, there is more than enough incentive for me to find the motivation to keep doing a good job for you."

DIVERSIFY IN *YOUR* COMPANY

Most owners I talk to say that if they had the opportunity

to not roll over anything, they would take it. They would simply take 100 percent of the proceeds at close. If you feel the same, I would like to challenge you.

The first thing that happens when an entrepreneur sells their company is they go buy a new house or car, or perhaps a boat or a nice vacation. They spend some of it, but then what? They have to look for investment opportunities. Why not your own company?

What's better than selling your company once? Selling it two, three, or even four times. My personal record is selling one company five times. That's five multimillion-dollar paydays over about a thirteen-year period.

And for each sale, a private equity firm is seeking a three-times return on their money invested (MOIC). They build a model, imagine a future, and determine what it will take to grow a business to get that return on investment in five years.

LAW OF ROLLOVER

Here's the law of rollover I suggest. When you sell a company, take sixty-six cents for every dollar home. Pay taxes, diversify your assets, and so forth. But if you're staying in the company, roll over thirty-four cents. Why thirty-four? If the private equity plans a three-times return on investment, thirty-four cents times three is $1.02. The second bite of the apple is actually larger than the first.

SIGNIFICANTLY INCREASE YOUR RETURN

In the last four years with CoolSys, I've bought eighteen companies. In the next four years, I'll buy another forty. This is a classic buy and build situation, and we're accelerating our efforts. We're putting dozens of companies together, and all of the entrepreneurs are still around. They are also all rollover investors.

As I mentioned in Chapter Two, we paid an early seller approximately $16 million for his business. He took $12 million home and rolled $4 million back into the company. Twenty-seven months later, I sold the company for four times the MOIC. His 25 percent rollover with a four-times return on investment meant he got another check for $16 million. It was as big as his first.

I asked the seller if he would have taken the first $16 million home if he could have. His response was, "Absolutely! I didn't value rollover investing, and I just hoped to get the $4 million back someday. I was required to do the rollover investing, but I would not have if given the option."

So what happened? After he got the second check for $16 million, he bought a winery but rolled over several million more for the next flip. He has now semi-retired and is making some fabulous wine, and we have another leader running his business, but he is still around and comes running from the hills if we need his help. He has gotten two bites of the apple already and has enough riding for round three to make it the largest payday of his career.

All of the other entrepreneurs who've also had multiple bites of the apple will tell you the same thing: rollover investing can be a great way to enhance your return while at the same time building diversity in your portfolio. Today in my current company, former owners and executive employees have over $42 million invested at CoolSys. We understand the power of rollover!

DON'T BE ARROGANT

Have you given up control? Absolutely. You have a new boss. But at the same time, the financial buyer is seeking to back you and is hoping you'll stay on and stay engaged. They want you to use their additional capital and expertise to build the business and then partake in the proceeds earned as a result.

It's arrogant to think that a business can't make money if you're not running it. Keep in mind that over the last thirty years, private equity has grown from zero to approximately $4 trillion in assets under management. The industry has grown from a few hundred firms twenty years ago to more than 6,000 firms today. These are very sophisticated people and generally earn twice what the stock market is earning. They have long track records of making outsized returns for their investors, and you get to ride their sophisticated coattails by becoming a rollover investor.

Rollover investing can create generational wealth. It's the ability to earn enough money that you won't be able to spend it in your lifetime—and your kids won't even be able to spend it in their lifetime! It's the opportunity to dig into philanthropic pursuits and build out your passions. So rollover investing is definitely something that you should consider in most strategic deals where you join the team instead of turning the lights out.

Across my twenty-year career, I have made an interesting observation. Entrepreneurs who can go from zero to a million in revenue are very rare. The DNA that makes them successful starts to encounter problems at around $20 million in revenue. These entrepreneurs are very controlling—it's what made them successful. In order to scale from $20 million to $100 million, their DNA needs to be altered. They need to trust in people and become conductors of the orchestra as opposed to the first chair player in each section. Those who can shift to a different gear and continue to scale are the rarest breed of all. Only 7 percent of entrepreneurs get to a million. Less than 5 percent of those get to a hundred million. Learning to partner is a powerful skill as you contemplate selling your company.

RESIDUAL INCOME STREAMS

There's always additional money to be made. Think of it like walking into a car dealership and purchasing a car. They make money off the sale, but they also try to sell you more. Extended factory warranty? Fabric protection? Gap insurance? Wheel locks? LoJack? They tack on these extras you can purchase. As a seller, you have additional residual income streams available too:

- Provide seller financing. When my brother Mike and I first bought the insurance agency I discussed earlier, the seller held back a $1 million note at 10 percent. The cash flow of the insurance agency paid it back over the next five years, but that former owner made the additional 10 percent for several years, and it was secured by the business being sold.
- Be a landlord. We've already discussed spinning your real estate off, and you can continue to be a landlord to the new business owner.
- Become a consultant. Many owners pivot to a consulting agreement with the new owner.

There are many different ways to maximize your potential in selling the business, but definitely don't discount the value of rollover or residual income streams.

KEY TAKEAWAYS

- Don't discount the value of rollover.

- Why sell once when you can sell twice?

- Consider other potential residual income streams.

CHAPTER THIRTEEN

↓

CHOOSING A WINNER

Throughout this book, the objective has been to educate you on the steps you need to take to prepare your business for sale, assemble your team, and navigate the sale process.

Now it's coming to an end, and you're faced with the last handful of potential buyers.

How do you decide? Is it just about price?

EMPLOYEES AND LEGACY

For most entrepreneurs, price is the absolute leading driver. And that's not wrong. There's no right or wrong here. But I've also encountered entrepreneurs who care very deeply about the employees who helped them build their business. And if presented with two buyers who are relatively close in price, one strategic and one financial, the entrepreneur might decide against a strategic buyer that is interested in turning the lights off and firing much of the staff.

That pains them and directs them to another buyer that may be offering a little less money.

So I suggest that you, the entrepreneur, need to think about this before you get into the sale process. What is important? What are you really trying to achieve? What legacy do you want to leave with the employees and families who have helped you over the years?

I've worked with entrepreneurs who were very generous. When we first divested a big piece of the business that I was running almost eighteen years ago, the founding entrepreneur gave up two years' salary to the employees. These people did not lose their jobs; they simply shifted from one owner to another. But the family distributed this money to the employees based on their tenure as a gesture of their gratitude for helping them be successful.

It was the most generous thing I had ever seen. But it's not something most people do. I recall another owner who felt that they had covered their employees' salaries over the years and that was fair enough. I've seen all points on the spectrum. Again, there's no right or wrong. It's just an element you need to consider. Like everything else we have discussed, the more prepared you are, the easier this process will be when it actually happens.

TIMING AND SURETY OF CLOSE

Another important consideration is your realistic view that a buyer can successfully close the transaction. When I ran the family-owned business, the family wanted to ride off into the sunset. We were selling to a financial buyer, and I had a fixed value number to hit in order for the family to agree to the sale. As we worked through the sales process, I had multiple financial buyers that looked at the business. It came down to two buyers. One was willing to write a check for the entire purchase price and get financing after the close. The other was willing to offer slightly more money, but it was contingent on financing. The delta was 1 percent, or $5 million.

The family went with the larger offer, and luckily the higher bid did close. However, I had to go out and help that party raise the capital. We had to find additional equity investors to come in alongside the original buyer, and it took time. Time is never your friend when you're selling a company. We were financed by GE Capital, and they wanted to delay the close. I kept pushing forward, and thank goodness I did! We closed on a Friday in August 2008, and the following week, the markets collapsed.

We did all of this for an extra $5 million and a significant layer of complexity around the financing. The funny part is that during diligence, the buyer negotiated the price down $5 million, so in reality, the closing value was the same as the other, more secure buyer. There was a real chance the deal would never close due to the added risk, but in this case, I got the job done.

Similar sales probably fell through during the pandemic of 2020. If a movie theater or restaurant chain was in a sales process early in the year, but a buyer needed thirty or sixty days to obtain financing, those sales likely fell apart when everyone went into quarantine.

Timing is everything. I've seen it happen twice now in my adult career where the market turned on a dime overnight and there were wide-ranging implications for a business that no one saw coming. When you're in this competitive process and getting down to the wire, you need to look a layer deeper than just price and determine who will give you the best surety of close.

KEY TAKEAWAYS

- Know in advance the future you seek for yourself.

- Price is important, but alignment is key to your future success.

- Decisions based solely on price have consequences.

- Time is not your friend. World-shifting events can happen at any time and without prior warning. When you are a seller, be a seller quickly and efficiently.

- Own and steer the process—don't just ride the wave!

PART FOUR WRAP-UP

In Part Four, we talked about creating marketing material, the typical competitive sale process flow and timeline, how to interact with buyers, rollover investing, and how to choose a winner.

I also want to note that during the sales process, your advisors will be more active in different phases. Your accounting advisor will help you prepare the business for sale in the years before the transaction and then will assist in diligence and perhaps after closing when it's time for any accounting true-ups for things like working capital adjustments. Your personal tax advisor will be active before the process begins to help you assess the impact to taxation based on the type of sale (asset versus stock) and the impact of where you reside. During the sale process, the personal tax advisor fades into the background, but they become prominent after closing as you deal with the actual tax burdens created when the windfall hits.

Your lawyer will be with you through the purchase process to represent you in negotiating any contracts and offer legal advice on any roadblocks that occur during diligence. Their role starts slowly but then picks up dramatically as diligence commences and contract negotiation begins. Their activity fades after close but may reactivate in spurts to deal with the post-closing true-ups and if any trailing liability issues arise.

The person you'll be spending the most time with during the sale process is your investment banker, who guides you through that sale process from start to finish.

CONCLUSION

In this book, we learned about the universe of buyers and the different types, their needs, and how they potentially fit with your goals. This doesn't mean you exclude any other buyers. In fact, competitive tension is good when you have multiple classes of buyers active.

We learned how and when to prepare a business for sale. Learn from the likes of private equity firms. They are the most sophisticated buyers on the planet.

We discussed the importance of building your advisory team. You need a tax advisor, both from a personal perspective and from a company perspective. You need a good accountant to help you with quality of earnings and normalize your accounting practices to make sure that they line up and that you're prepared for diligence. You need expert legal advice because selling your company is most likely the biggest transaction that you will ever have in your life. And of course, you need the expertise of an investment banker to help you through the process.

We talked about the sales process itself. Now when a banker discusses fireside chats and CIPs, they won't just be Scrabble words. They'll hold meaning for you.

Armed with this information, you are set up for a higher probability of success in monetizing your life's work and sailing off to your next adventure.

Don't hesitate to reach out on LinkedIn or on the web at www.AdamECoffey.com. I always love hearing from readers. And if a financial buyer is in the mix, read The Private Equity Playbook to learn more about what an adventure with private equity really looks like.

ACKNOWLEDGMENTS

No book is possible without the help and contributions of many people. I'd like to take a moment to acknowledge and thank some of them here.

Nikki Katz, my personal writing coach and mentor. Without her technical guidance and creativity, my effort would amount to a warm pile of drivel.

Tim Lappen, Partner, Founder, and Chairman of the Family Office Group and Luxury Home Group at Jeffer Mangels Butler and Mitchell in Los Angeles. His legal advice and friendship have always been of tremendous value when writing my books.

Karan Aggarwal, my VP of Corporate Development at Cool-Sys. There are times in life when the mentor gets schooled by the mentee, and although I am not a CPA in life—or on TV—he is one of the finest I have had the pleasure to work with and whose brain I raided for some technical advice while writing this book.

Mike Coffey, my brother, business partner, best man, and best friend. We seem to have garnered the majority of the family's business DNA and were the two who followed our father's footsteps into corporate America and succeeded in becoming multimillionaires, CEOs, and business owners.

All the professionals at the various private equity firms and investment banks I have had the privilege to work with during my twenty-year adventure in private equity—far too many to enumerate here individually. It wasn't always easy or smooth, but it sure was rewarding and a lot of fun! I learned from you all and am thankful for the opportunities you provided.

ABOUT THE AUTHOR

ADAM COFFEY has spent twenty years as president and CEO of three national service companies, all in different industries. In each case, Adam was at the helm for multiple shareholder groups as the businesses grew, raised capital, and changed hands.

Adam's first company, Masterplan, was a medical device service company owned by Three Cities Research (NYC) and Camden Partners (Baltimore) that was subsequently sold after his departure to Berkshire Partners (Boston) in 2007 and later became a division of Aramark (NYSE: ARMK) in 2011.

Adam's second company, WASH Multifamily Laundry, a commercial laundry service company, started as a family-owned business that was subsequently sold to Code Hennessy &

Simmons (Chicago) in 2008 and then again to EQT Partners (Stockholm) in 2015.

Adam currently leads his third company, CoolSys, a commercial refrigeration and HVAC service company. Adam was hired by the Audax Group (Boston) in 2016, and in 2019 he led the sale to Ares Management (NYSE: ARES).

Known for building strong employee-centered cultures and for executing a buy and build strategy, Coffey is highly sought after by private equity and is considered an expert in running industrial service businesses. Adam is a former GE executive, an alumnus of the UCLA Anderson Executive Program, a pilot, and a veteran of the US Army. He is married, a father of three, and makes his home in Westlake, Texas. Adam can be found on LinkedIn at www.linkedin.com/in/adamecoffey or via his website www.AdamECoffey.com.

Made in the USA
Las Vegas, NV
30 August 2023

76839088R00121